LEGAL
TERRORISM

The truth about the Christic Institute

TABLE OF CONTENTS

ACKNOWLEDGEMENTS

"Thanks" of a sort are due to Professor Daniel Premo, Chair-critter of the Department of Political Science at the Chestertown Brain Laundry, a.k.a. Washington College, without whose barrage of propaganda I might have missed the Christics.

Seriously, when the Christic lawsuit charging anti-Communists with "criminal racketeering" was thrown out of court in Miami in June of 1988, I wrote an article on the subject for *Conservative Digest* (October, 1988). It was partly inspired by Cliff Kincaid's work in *Human Events* and by David Brock's very fine piece in *The American Spectator,* all of which had demonstrated the scope of the problem.

Becoming acquainted with "the major defendants" made the outrageous nature of the Christic assault even clearer. They were trapped in a no-win situation by clever use of a tough law called RICO, aimed against organized crime. They were victims of a political vendetta fueled by tax-free foundation and church money, with a big boost from the mass media.

They were chosen *because* they were retired, and would thus be left to face huge legal bills on their own. The effect was described by one defendant as similar to a catastrophic illness! The Christics tell us that they planned it that way.

Having seen my *Conservative Digest* article, the Christics would not part with any information. "Is Sara Nelson from Oklahoma?" drew a zipped lip. However, I was greatly assisted by many people, some of whom would rather remain unmentioned. Robert "Gus" Breene provided much background and information on people and events in Central America, and offers his own moderately-priced publications with more detail. (Write to him at Suite 216, 2186 Jackson Keller, San Antonio, TX 78213.)

Ned Dolan is an enthusiastic Washington-area radical-watcher, a mine of interesting items and connections. Columnist Pat Buchanan offered a key tip, and Ernest Lefevre helped me to "get oriented" in the world of mainline Protestantism and the National and World Councils of Churches. Robert Campbell of *The Presbyterian Layman* was also helpful in this respect. Both gentlemen are tough fighters against the hijacking of the churches by radicals

2

using them for political purposes.

Mike Mangiameli of Robeson County, North Carolina, defends his county and its people with a clear eye, a stout heart, and the kind of no-nonsense attitude one tends to associate with reporters in the "classic" tradition.

Bill Poole of the Capital Research Center in Washington offered the results of his own research into foundations, and tips on digging for information in that field.

Dr. Petr Beckmann aided in debunking the massive misinformation put forth by lawyers in the Silkwood case.

Finally, the usual caveat—none of the above individuals are in any way responsible for any errors which may appear.

Thanks also to Freda Fenwick, Sarah Edwards, and Frannie Bakeoven, who helped to make available the time needed to write this book.

Susan Huck
22 October, 1989

INTRODUCTION

The headlines worldwide scream about terrorism. We hear about Euro-terrorism, alias Action Direct, Communist Fighting Cells, the Red Brigades, Red Army Fraction and the Baader-Meinhof gang, to mention a few. Narco-terrorism is a new catchword which rivets our attention on the Medellin Cartel and M-19 guerrillas in Colombia. The household words of the Middle East, such as Intifada, Hezbollah, PLO, PFLP, PFLP-GC and Abu Nidal, constantly ring in our ears from television and radio programs. Yet little is being said or done about the American phenomenon called "legal terrorism."

We define legal terrorism as a form of political warfare. It does not place one life in imminent danger of death or dismemberment. What it does do is to ruin the target's life. This is done by the law and through the courts.

The objective of legal terrorism is to set a political agenda via the courts. The methodology used by legal terrorists results in politically motivated civil suits and the civil provisions of the Racketeer Influenced and Corrupt Organizations Act (RICO) being harnessed to discredit honorable men. When the terrorists strike, the equivalent for the victim in terms of loss of time and money is the same as what happens when a catastrophic illness hits a family.

Unlike the situation in many parts of the world where the victim does not know his attackers, we know who is at fault. The current primary practitioner of legal terrorism is the Christic Institute, 1324 North Capital Street, N.W., Washington, DC 20002, a tax-exempt 501(c)(3) corporation. This self-described "liberal church-funded law group" has since May 1986 entangled thirty or more people in a RICO lawsuit, Avirgan *vs.* Hull *et al*, charging the defendants with membership in a murderous, drug smuggling "secret team" of anti-Communists and a "shadow government" engaged in off-the-shelf operations. These false claims forced people to put their lives on hold, to hear themselves vilified in the media, and to defend their rights at great cost.

The true merits of this case were revealed on June 23, 1988 when Judge James Lawrence King of Miami granted summary judgments to all defendants by dismissing the case. Judge King wrote in his opinion that the Christics' two year investigation had failed to produce any facts and their case was without merit.

The court subsequently awarded the defendants a Rule 11 judgment which required the posting of a supersedeas bond for a little more than 1.2 million dollars as the Christic Institute and their plaintiffs had filed a case "based upon unsubstantiated rumor and speculation from unidentified sources with no first hand knowledge." The Christics have this matter and the summary judgment on appeal with the Eleventh Circuit Court of Appeals in Atlanta.

Not content with the havoc they had created in *Avirgan vs. Hull,* the Christics became involved with Robeson County, North Carolina. This case involves the February 1, 1988 takeover of *The Robesonian* newspaper by Eddie Hatcher and Timothy Jacobs while armed with sawed-off shotguns. The bottom line is that while trying to defend Hatcher and Jacobs, particularly the latter, the Christics engaged in actions which subsequently caused the North Carolina Attorney General's office to file a motion in U.S. District Court asking for Rule 11 sanctions against a Christic lawyer and others. The Court ruled on September 29, 1989 that the Christic lawyer, Lewis Pitts, and others had violated Rule 11. The attorneys were thus penalized for introducing frivolous or groundless lawsuits during the Hatcher-Jacobs trials.

We know of no other legal group in America that has been sanctioned twice under Rule 11 procedures in an eight-month period. That tells one something about the Christic Institute's credibility and professionalism.

It is anticipated the Christics will continue to practice their brand of legal terrorism. They will make charges of corruption, drug smuggling and murder against other people and will stubbornly refuse to identify witnesses while dishing out contemptuous treatment to judges. Just as matching fingerprints and DNA genetic-typing help identify criminals, this behavior pattern will help journalists recognize the Christic Institute or its clones in whatever guise or under whatever name they may appear. This book therefore is dedicated to the task of putting the spotlight of reason on "legal terrorism" so that issues of national security policy can be resolved at the ballot box or by open debate rather than through concocted material being introduced into the courts.

CHAPTER ONE

SETTING THE STAGE

What is "legal terrorism"? Well, it is not the sort of terrorism which places one in imminent danger of death or dismemberment. It's legal—it is done by and through the law. If successful, it can ruin your life and impoverish your family.

One of the heaviest weapons now available to legal terrorists is the Racketeer Influenced and Corrupt Organizations, or RICO, statute, designed for use against organized crime. It is available for the pursuit of private, civil lawsuits as well as criminal cases. Thus, it is available to anyone who wants to try using it. And many aspects of RICO are a striking and frightening departure from previous legal norms, as we shall see.

When a legal terrorist says, "We're going to take everything they have, and put them in jail for the rest of their lives," and has millions of dollars with which to try, the victim will know a species of terror. Even if innocent, he can be ruined by legal costs alone—and if he can't afford a good lawyer, he may not be found innocent, either!

Legal terrorism is becoming a form of political warfare, and a prime example is the La Penca RICO case, now on appeal. Pinned to a bomb attack at La Penca on the Nicaraguan border in 1984 is a civil racketeering case involving false charges on a truly grand scale. The "major defendants" were chosen for political reasons.

In an article appearing in the September/October 1989 issue of *Chief Executive* magazine, the matter was put succinctly:

> The *Wall Street Journal* recently noted that both civil and criminal

RICO cases may be blatantly political. The occasion was the imposition, last February, of Rule 11 sanctions against lawyer Daniel Sheehan and his two plaintiffs, Anthony Avirgan and Martha Honey. Rule 11 of the Federal Code of Civil Procedure is intended to give pause to lawyers filing frivolous or unfounded suits, by holding them liable for the defendants' attorney fees and court costs.

In the case of Sheehan, Avirgan, and Honey, this came to $1,034,381.36.

The article sketched the La Penca lawsuit, which was filed by a tax-exempt entity, the Christic Institute, self-described as "an interfaith center for law and public policy."

The *New York Times,* on March 17, 1989, voiced some small concern "about what kind of evidentiary thread is woven through the Christics' tapestry of allegations that a 'secret team' of veterans of the Central Intelligence Agency, Cuban exiles, and soldiers of fortune spent thirty continent-hopping years dealing in drugs, arms, death, and anti-Communism."

Guess which the Christics believe is the *real* crime.

The lawsuit actually contends that men like retired Army Major General John Singlaub and retired senior CIA official Theodore Shackley had been acting on their own throughout their careers—since 1959, in fact—that they had hoodwinked the government into paying their salaries, while they were *really* engaged in a global racketeering enterprise of awesome scope.

The La Penca lawsuit is awesome in its own way. It is a misrepresentation, on a truly staggering scale, of what these men have been doing all their lives. Basically, the Christics are trying to convince the public—and, if possible, the court—that fighting the Communists is nothing but a criminal activity.

A check of the Soviet penal code will find a congruent view.

Who on earth, one may well ask, could possibly take these contentions seriously? Well, even a federal judge cannot prevent a case from entering the judicial system. Once in the system, a clever lawyer can drag it out for years. If money is not a problem, dragging it out may be the best thing he can do with it.

And money is no problem for the Christic Institute. Its La Penca lawsuit has been such a popular item in leftist circles that Institute income has tripled, from $832,000 in 1986 to $2,622,000 in 1988. The Jane Fonda types can't get enough of this story—nor can the hierarchs of the mainline churches, as it happens. The money just rolls in, at a rate of $50,000 a week, from people who share the passionate hope that the Christics can actually brand armed resistance to Communism a criminal racketeering conspiracy!

We shall meet the people involved—the plaintiffs, and key personnel of the Christic Institute. Then we shall meet "the major defendants," and it will become apparent that the lawsuit represents an assault by adherents of an ideology against those with quite different views and values. But the attack really aims at even larger targets—the institutions of the Presidency and the Central Intelligence Agency, the principle of covert action, and American foreign policy objectives in Central America.

We shall look at the tactics employed, and study in depth the surprisingly large support network backing the legal terrorists—their media allies, the foundations which fuel the attack, even the churches whose officials find ways to help out.

And finally, we shall attempt to answer the question, "Why do they do it?"

Theodore Shackley, one of the targeted "major defendants" and an author and lecturer on national security topics, has tried to analyze and define "legal terrorism":

> The objective is to set a political agenda via the courts. The
> methodology . . . is to embroil principals or surrogates in civil
> lawsuits through the use of false claims and concocted testimony
> in order to set the stage for a public relations campaign which
> will sensationalize issues of interest to the instigators . . .

That Daniel Sheehan and his associates at the Christic Institute have a political agenda is obvious and beyond question. It is revealed in their own statements, not to speak of their actions, and it is verified by the company they keep. From this perspective, attacking "principals or surrogates" means attacking either the people you really mean to attack, or, if they are unavailable, then attacking "surrogates," substitutes, subordinates or stand-ins who will have to do. We have seen it in the Oliver North trial, where North was a surrogate for Ronald Reagan, in the eyes of many.

There are plenty of surrogates for both Ronald Reagan and George Bush in the civil RICO suit brought by Sheehan. The chosen defendants, the CIA as a foreign policy tool, and covert action as a foreign policy method, are attacked instead of the Presidency.

In a California speech, Sheehan said as much: "The method we are using now, going after 29 people, is a tactical step. Because the minute you move on the President . . . you get all this resistance, assertions that we're being unpatriotic or communists . . ."

"False claims and concocted testimony" come cheap, heaven knows. They can even be tax-exempt. We shall make the acquaintance of those who grab a tax deduction by paying for "false witness"—a list which includes some who distribute money collected from church congregations nationwide.

The "campaign which will sensationalize issues of interest to the instigators" is a major purpose of the lawsuit, although wreaking vengeance on principals or surrogates is a pleasure which legal terrorists do not deny themselves, as the "fingered" defendants are very well aware.

Shackley continues:

> The unwitting handmaidens of the legal terrorists are the media,
> and the overburdened courts, which are unable or unwilling to
> deal, in a timely manner, with suits that are patently without merit.

With respect to the media, the word "unwitting" gives to many the benefit of the doubt. The straight news media—newspapers, magazines, and television—either appreciate the sensational charges as a way "to sell papers" and regard denials as a predictable bore, or avert their eyes from the lynching under way.

Beyond the news media, we find a full panoply of media of communications capable of reaching the minds of the American people and implanting selected information and attitudes. All too many of the people who decide what five, forty, or one hundred million Americans are going to see, "learn," or "know" by the end of the day have their own political agenda, and it may very well happen to mesh with that of the legal terrorists.

Certainly, a civil lawsuit in Miami would not be announced at the National Press Club in Washington if the impresario expected to be met with skepticism, indifference, and even derision. Rather, the expectation is that a substantial number of those present will grab the ball and run with it toward a mutually understood goal line.

As for the courts, historically it has been left to members of the legal profession to prescribe for their ailments. But there is no doubt that the system is "overburdened," clogged with cases, and glacially slow in reaching decisions—decisions often regarded as bizarre by the citizenry at large, by the way.

In conclusion, Shackley points out:

> This permits the legal terrorist to harness the inertia of the courts
> to use the 'window of opportunity' between the filing of an
> outrageous suit and its dismissal . . . to raise funds, pump invec-

tive against their targets into the media, and focus attention on issues that have previously been decided or are out of the mainstream of American political life.

A sensational lawsuit—meaning sensational charges against well-known people (or their luckless surrogates, who soon enough become household words)—makes for great fund-raising opportunities. This is especially so if it has already been arranged that donations are tax-deductible. In this manner, wealthy celebrities can fight their fashionable political battles while obtaining a big tax break from Uncle Sam.

Literally millions of dollars have been hauled in from these and other sources to finance a lawsuit which gives new meaning to the word "shameless."

The pumping of invective against selected defendants, for years on end, mocks the "presumption of innocence." False charges can be spread by every means, and the victims are virtually without recourse. The Christics have made millions, literally, out of their own propaganda. At the same time, the sheer volume of it converts the defendants into "public figures," who, as a result, have almost no chance of winning a libel suit, under current American law.

Covert Cadre

In 1987, a truly remarkable book was produced—*Covert Cadre,* by journalist Scott Stephen Powell. Focusing on the Institute for Policy Studies, which is usually described as a "liberal think tank" in Washington, he revealed the scope, the funding, and the orientation of what is actually the center of a gigantic spider web of left-leaning influence.

What kind of influence? What does IPS do—and on whose behalf? Powell knows very well, and said so as clearly as he dared, by referring to the 16th Century poet John Harington.

As he observed, "Treason doth never prosper. What's the reason? Why, if it prosper, none dare call it treason." If the traitors win, then no one, mindful of his head, had better note that their activities were actually treasonous. The traitors themselves become the judges of that.

Undoubtedly, Powell knows that *None Dare Call It Treason* was the title of one of three books, published in 1964, which sold three to six million copies apiece. In the view of the Liberal Establishment, they should not have existed; therefore, they "did not exist."

Despite the fact that any publisher would have made a mint on them, each had to be printed by the author. Each was denied any form of normal distribution. Each was ignored by the Establishment as long as possible—and, when this was no longer possible, treated with unalloyed scorn. Political science students, looking at the extremely interesting 1964 election campaign, are routinely denied knowledge of the existence of these books, and have a close to zero chance of finding them.

The subject of treason has been declared out of bounds, but Powell defies that ban.

His book contains an extremely revealing introduction by David Horowitz, son of Communists, and a long-time Communist himself—a New Left son of the Old Left. He points out that his parents and their entire circle of friends appeared to be ordinary middle-class people, idealists, of course—but that they considered themselves soldiers of the revolution, and accepted with pleasure and without reservation whatever orders came from Moscow. "[To] break faith with the Soviet rulers, or to weaken the instruments of Soviet power, would be to betray everything important to them in their lives. They would rather have betrayed their country. . ."

And they did.

Among those Red friends, Horowitz notes, was Cora Weiss. She is the daughter of Samuel Rubin, a longtime Communist who appropriated the name of Faberge from its owners, refugees from the Soviet dictatorship, and made a fortune with products bearing their name. He dedicated that fortune to the support of Communist activities in the United States.

Rubin's money is a revealing thread connecting groups or organizations serving Communist goals in the United States. Powell's "covert cadre" consists of key personnel in these groups—interlocking leadership, members transferred among the cluster of groups, those trained within the groups and then sent out to expand the network.

Unlike corporate donors, who may be inattentive, not to say criminally negligent, about what their money supports, Rubin's money deliberately goes to groups conducting activities in which the Communists have a considered interest.

Cora Weiss may also be remembered from Vietnam days.

Suppose that, during World War II, the loved ones of American prisoners of war had been publicly urged to contact a woman of open pro-Nazi sympathies, if they desired to communicate with their men. Suppose they had been urged, as the price of this contact, to push the Nazi propaganda line, become activists for their cause.

Unthinkable.

But then, we must remember, America's Liberals were not on Hitler's side. World War II was the last war they ever wanted to see through to victory. Since 1945, our punches have been pulled. It is part of the picture that treason has been tolerated.

Some day, someone will dust off Article III, Section 3 of the United States Constitution, where treason is defined.

Some of the finest citizens of our country are on trial, or threatened with trial for what our Establishment seems to regard as overzealousness in resistance to Communist expansion. At the same time, turncoats roam free, and the scum of America are granted the unfettered right to defile the symbols and values of our national being.

In his summation, Powell states that his purpose has been "to document the ideas and activities of the [IPS] and its associates in the context of their bearing on the political culture, public opinion, and policy-making in the United States."

The Christic Institute is simply another arm of the very large radical incubus in America. The Christics are engaged in the same basic effort as the Institute for Policy Studies.

CHAPTER TWO

AVIRGAN AND HONEY

The plaintiffs in the La Penca racketeering lawsuit are Anthony Avirgan and Martha Honey, husband and wife, both now in their middle forties. Tony Avirgan was born in Philadelphia in 1944, and Martha Honey in Orange, N.J. in 1945.

The Christics say that Avirgan "attended" Penn State, which is all he did. He received no degree. While of college age, he says he was a "professional motorcycle racer," and later a "market research consultant." He finally found himself as an anti-war demonstrator and "organizer," working with "New Mobe."

That was the then-current term by which the "Mobilization" committee running demonstrations against the Vietnam War was known. In September 1966, a committee was formed, which became known as the Spring Mobilization Committee to End the War in Vietnam. After its activities in early 1967 were completed, the name was changed to National Mobilization Committee to End the War in Vietnam, and the shortened handle of "Mobe" became attached to it.

It was "Mobe" which brought us the 1968 riots at the Democratic National Convention in Chicago. (In typical left-wing usage, these were turned around and called "police riots,"—and in typical me-too fashion, media liberals picked up the line.) Yet another convention on the Fourth of July, 1969, brought forth another incarnation of the Committee, which was thereafter known as New Mobe.

Every incarnation of Mobe was dominated by the American left-wing.

The guiding lights were often known members of the Communist Party, USA. Back in those days, Congress had a House Internal Security Committee which looked into these things and actually listed the Communist Party members. That's before the Communists and their "liberal" allies were strong enough to assert, successfully, that the Communists weren't the threat, the House Committee was the threat!

Avirgan probably joined "Mobe" about 1968. By February, 1970, he was listed as a headquarters *apparatchik* in Washington. This is not to say that he was a member of the Communist Party, USA. This is to say that he accepted Communist leadership, and served them satisfactorily.

Martha Honey graduated from Oberlin College in 1967. The College, then and now, was a dense nest of Trotskyites—the "Trots" normally meet at Oberlin, and a goodly portion of the faculty sign on as sponsors of the gatherings. Martha then began her career as a radical in Philadelphia, as a "youth director" with the Friends' Peace Committee, and "researcher" for NARMIC, National Action/Research on the Military-Industrial Complex. In Philadelphia, she met Tony—which was awkward, as she had just married one Peter Westover. But that was easily remedied; she divorced Westover in 1969, but retained the Westover name until 1971.

At the time of her divorce, she was also enrolled at Syracuse University, where her father was a professor of political science. He was affiliated with the Maxwell School of Public Administration. The School was then, and probably still is, packed wall-to-wall with believers in Planning with a capital P. Maxwell was intended as a training ground for economic and social planners of the New Deal stripe.

Daughter Martha was carried on the books at Syracuse as a "research associate," which seemed to leave her a great deal of free time, since she was able to live with Tony in Philadelphia and work for "peace groups."

Tony stayed out of military service with an ooh-my-back problem, a souvenir of motorcycle racing days which left him borderline 4-F. But he "refused to accept" that, because he was counseling draft-dodgers, you see, and felt he could not do this with a 4-F card in his pocket. So someone decided okay, he could be 1-A (instant draft-bait) and how did that grab him?

He didn't care for that, either. He objected, and "some big law firm in Philadelphia" took his case, his mother says. "He was under indictment, you know, for several years." But, in the end, the government did nothing.

The "New Mobe" leadership found Tony's work most satisfactory—and Martha Westover's, too. As a reward, both were given a free trip to Hanoi in August of 1970. No, they did not stay at the "Hanoi Hilton," where the other Americans, our POWs, were accommodated. In fact, they evidenced zero concern for the other Americans in Hanoi.

What did capture their imagination was reflected in an article they wrote entitled "From Hanoi, with Love." The lovers found Hanoi heavenly. No poverty—everybody gets his pound of rice a day (period). No vice, no crime—the police were unarmed pussycats, not like the American Blue Meanies. No unhappiness. "People are generally smiling and you just don't see fights or arguments . . . the atmosphere in Hanoi is the kind you used to feel on some U.S. campuses or youth sections of cities before things turned ugly. . ."

"We spent our first few days in meetings, reporting on our interpretation of the current situation in the U.S. and the state of the U.S. movement. The Vietnamese were quite interested in this as the future of their country greatly depends on developments in the U.S. and they took very careful notes. We were all impressed about how much they knew about the U.S. movement, even to the point of knowing all the latest movement gossip."

Hanoi considered it "intel," of course. Giving that sort of intelligence to the enemy in time of war is treason. But, we are to believe, Vietnam was not a war. It had every earmark of a war but the legal one—a Congressional declaration of war—so Avirgan and Honey were "home free," just like "Hanoi Jane" Fonda. They differ only in their lack of celebrity.

"Hanoi Jane" will wear her favorite scent, *puanteur de trahison,* stench of treason, for life. Avirgan and Honey deserve no less.

They spent about two weeks in North Vietnam, receiving the usual speeches-and-flowers treatment. Once, they were unnerved when they were led into a place where a mutilated woman hugged them; their guides' explanation was that she had been mutilated by American bombs, and Tony and Martha were the first Americans she had ever seen, and her natural inclination was, therefore, to embrace them . . .

If it was a test of credulity—will they swallow anything if it comes from a Communist source?—they passed.

Like Jane Fonda, they were sent home with a "beautiful" souvenir inscribed "made from the metal of the first plane of the U.S. air pirates shot down . . ."

It is clear that Martha and Tony tried hard to please their Communist patrons, at home and abroad. They succeeded, and made a career of it. Why not? You can make a career of it.

Martha's "researches" brought her a master's degree from Syracuse in 1971, and she married Tony in September.

Tony tried even harder to please the Communists. He signed a public "statement of responsibility," boasting of having sabotaged three C-130 transports at the Willow Grove Naval Air Station on Memorial Day, 1972. The "hydraulic and electrical lines" they cut were probably in the landing gear, the most accessible place.

Our government never did anything about it, probably because Tony's word wasn't good enough.

In 1973, Martha Honey received a foundation grant, believed to be from Shell Oil, to study "the Asian community in Tanzania and Zanzibar." The young scholar was inaccurate here. Zanzibar's moment of independence ended with the creation of Tanzania, a merger of Tanganyika and Zanzibar. The island (actually, a pair of islands) was independent for one historic heartbeat before being swallowed.

The interim "liberator" of Zanzibar was named John Okello, whose radio broadcasts enlivened the otherwise sleep-inducing pages of "the Fibs," published by FBIS, which stands for Foreign Broadcast Information Service. The U.S. government captures and transcribes an enormous volume of foreign broadcast material, and then publishes, every day, what amounts to a book-length collection of the tirades of tyrants, the dronings of spokesmen, the boasts of revolutionaries, comprising much of what has been "on the air" in recent days. Picking through this mass of verbiage for the occasional valuable gem of needed information is a dismal job.

The author had occasion to be reading this material in 1964, when Comrade Okello was in power, and therefore some of his utterances remain at hand. For example:

> "Come and see how we hang people and burn them like chickens . . . Others will be sliced into little pieces . . . Others will be thrown into the sea, or tied to trees to be used for target practice by my novice marksmen . . . I would like to inform Hilali Kahenga that I want to see him hang himself. First he must kill all his children by slashing them with knives . . ."

Such is the unmentioned face of "liberation." Comrade Okello may not have lasted long enough to dispose of the entire "Asian community" of Zanzibar, so perhaps there was something left for Martha to study. (Actually, she said she was interested in Indians and Pakistanis, not Arabs, but neither group of Asians have had a happy time under the new African dictatorships.)

In any event, Avirgan and Honey went to Dar es-Salaam, capital of Tanzania, and relied upon her grant money for the period 1973 to 1975, which was quite a generous arrangement. It may owe something to her father's influence. The pair remained there for some ten years, serving as free-lance journalists for the leftist and "liberal" press.

They were particularly keen to home in on the destruction of nearby Rhodesia. They were quite able to overlook the massive unhappiness and disruption caused by their host, Tanzanian President Julius Nyerere, in his own country. They were present during the notorious "villagization" program, under which millions of Tanzanians were forced to burn down their own homes and relocate in non-existent "villages" where "social services" would be "delivered" in classic socialist-planning fashion.

Martha's father probably would have loved the entire concept. The reality, which so rarely intrudes upon the contemplations of socialist academics, was that the driven masses of humanity could consider themselves fortunate indeed to find so much as a well at the site of their assigned new utopian "village."

The true results in Tanzania were certainly not about to be reported by Avirgan and Honey, but they are visible, even reading between the lines of World Bank reports. Nyerere made his country poorer than ever before. Of a waspish nature, he berated the rest of the world for Tanzania's condition, with the result that he was given more and more money, eventually coming in second only to Israel in per-capita largesse received. And the entire program was called "self-reliance."

For this reason, Nyerere has been called "the dean of the Abusive school of mendicancy."

Christic sources like to say that Tony was "stationed" in Dar. They do not say, "stationed" by whom. The implication is that he was an employee of a large news organization, whereas he always was and is now a free-lancer and a stringer. Nothing wrong with that, but "stationed" is just not the word.

Nobody "stations" or "assigns" a free-lancer or stringer. Could it be that Avirgan and Honey have an employer they are not telling us about?

The Avirgan-Honey team sent news stories from Dar es-Salaam to far-left and "liberal" publications and broadcast groups, and also endeared themselves to Tanzania's dictator, Nyerere. Other journalists present in Dar at the same time thought they knew how Nyerere was kept informed about their views and intentions, and the communal finger was pointed in the direction of Avirgan and Honey.

No surprise, therefore, that Avirgan and Honey were granted "scoops" not available to others. This included allowing the American leftists to accompany Nyerere's plundering rabble on its invasion and "liberation" of Uganda. The same duo was also afforded a box seat from which to cheer the destruction of Rhodesia, which has now been converted into a one-party dictatorship using "comrade" as the title of address.

The Christic Institute tendency has been to emphasize the "respectable" press in the United States and Great Britain, which bought material from Avirgan and Honey, and to neglect to mention Avirgan's "Special to the *Guardian*" dispatches. The New York *Guardian*—well, let some of its problems be described, and then you decide what to call it.

While Avirgan was having his material published in the *Guardian*, it was running an emergency fund-raising effort. It was desperate. You see, the Chinese Communists had been most helpful, by purchasing 35,000 copies of every issue, and also by allowing the *Guardian* to monopolize tours of China by Americans. But then the paper tripped up, and followed the Moscow rather than the Beijing line on Cambodia. Punishment was instant. Financial problems resulted, until Cuba picked up the burden.

But it is really better to have Americans pay for their own brainwash. The *Guardian* is now a tax-exempt entity, and subscribers can take a deduction. Life in the left lane can be remarkably smooth.

Fran Avirgan, Tony's mother, testifies that Martha and her son lived very well in Dar; sharing the poverty is strictly for peasants. Nevertheless, they all decamped in 1983 and moved to San Jose, Costa Rica. Mrs. Avirgan described this as a logical shift of locale—a nice place to raise children, no army, calm—but lots of news in the area. The Christics say they were "given a new assignment" in Costa Rica. By whom?

At the last moment, Martha picked up a doctorate from the University of Dar es-Salaam—Julius K. Nyerere, Proprietor. At least she doesn't flaunt the degree.

Costa Rica

Jack Cox, a writer long familiar with Central America, is aware of the image which Costa Rica has enjoyed as a beautiful, peaceful, democratic little country—an image not far off the mark of truth for many years. But the advent of a Marxist Nicaragua next door has changed things a great deal. The "new," but hardly improved, San Jose, capital of Costa Rica, Cox compared to Lisbon during World War II—a "neutral" capital of bloated embassy staffs, teeming with spies, agents, and refugees:

> Costa Rica has become a political hotbed. An estimated 200,000 refugees from Nicaragua have poured into the country. The Soviet presence is considerable, and their agents are everywhere. The United States also has more people in Costa Rica than ever before. Marxist Sandinistas have entered the country and infiltrated many of the anti-Sandinista organizations. . . San Jose parks are now unsafe. One is advised to stay off the streets at night. Businesses and businessmen are easy targets for robbery. Physical assault is not uncommon. The cost of living has soared. All foreigners are suspect. For a country as small as Costa Rica [population then about 2.7 million], an influx of 200,000 Nicaraguans is tantamount to an invasion.

This is not a happy situation for either *ticos* or *nicas*. The refugees are burdensome and sometimes troublesome "guests," and they, too, would rather go home—but not to the present Sandinista management of their country.

No liberal wants to tell you about the manner in which both the United States and Costa Rica connived to guarantee the Sandinistas victory over the Somoza government. Through Jack Cox, Somoza told his side of things in *Nicaragua Betrayed,* and Cox notes, on page 163 of *Requiem in the Tropics,* the manner in which Costa Rica allowed its territory to be used by the Sandinistas. There is more in Whalen and Jaeckle's *The Soviet Assault on America's Southern Flank.*

Thus, Costa Rican shrieks of outraged neutrality hit the usual false note. What was done in the way of providing "hospitality" for the contras was no more than was offered to the Sandinistas in their previous turn.

It was in this milieu that Avirgan and Honey set up shop, still as free-lancers and stringers—and they were soon making a remarkably, or suspiciously, good living at it. When accused of consorting with Soviet officials, they say they are, after all, journalists. When their privileged position with regard to the Sandinista government is noted, they see nothing wrong with basking in the favor of the *comandantes*. It is good business, as it was good business with the dictators of East Africa.

The Southern Front

"The southern front" is a rather grandiose name for an effort which was rendered abortive by our home-front fifth column. The Carter Administration had bequeathed to a grateful nation a new Cuba—Nicaragua under Communist rule. And there was also the ceaseless Communist attempt to grab El Salvador. We Americans had, we thought, elected a new leadership team in 1980. However, the old fifth column still held a strong position in Washington, D.C. and in the media, and American fifth columnists are very good at their work, which is demoralization and subversion.

Of course, they have advantages which are available nowhere else on earth. No other government would tolerate such activities.

Many who had fought against Somoza felt betrayed by the Marxists in the Sandinista movement and decided to express their opposition by armed attacks against the Sandinista forces. On the first anniversary of the Sandinista take-over, they launched the first military attacks. One year later, in mid-1981, the Reagan Administration authorized the Central Intelligence Agency to organize, train, and support the FDN, or Nicaraguan Democratic Front. One side calls them freedom-fighters and the other calls them contras. While the author dislikes accepting enemy terminology, *contra* merely means "against," and is a good deal more convenient a term to use.

The Christics complain that the Reagan Administration failed to inform the world of this covert operation "for more than six months." That seems like a more than average lifespan for any American "secret" these days.

The main contra effort was in the north, along the Nicaraguan border with Honduras—and well into Nicaragua itself, let us not forget. The FDN were having some success in the field, despite the effectiveness of the fifth column here at home.

However, the CIA then decided that pressure from the south, from the Costa Rican side of Nicaragua, ought to work as well against the Sandinistas as it had against Somoza. But Somoza never had an American fifth column on his side.

And so it happened that the stirrings of a southern front coincided with the arrival in San Jose of Avirgan and Honey, experienced propagandists, self-admitted saboteurs and political activists. Would there be any question as to where their loyalties lay?

There wasn't much question at the American Embassy in San Jose. The CIA station chief says he filed reports on their activities. Author Robert "Gus" Breene studied the expenses run up by Avirgan and Honey while resident in Costa Rica, and concluded that they had an outside income. He states that a Costa Rican intelligence official noted more or less weekly meetings between them and Valentin B. Chekanov, whose KGB cover position, Breene says, was Press Secretary at the Soviet Embassy. It is, after all, a position frequently used as cover, according to KGB defectors.

As for the creation of a southern front, the potential leadership of Eden Pastora was available—more or less. Pastora had been a celebrated Sandinista, but was aced out of the position of Minister of Defense by Daniel Ortega's brother Humberto, whom Ortega seemed to consider more trustworthy. Pastora decided that the revolution had been betrayed, and took his talents elsewhere.

Pastora has always enjoyed a suspiciously favorable press, even when he was supposed to be a contra leader, and even after he was revealed as having been on the CIA payroll, which is normally the kiss of death in media circles.

La Penca: The Bombing

It began as a typical "pseudo-event" of the sort which journalists routinely waste their lives attending—an occurrence which would never have taken place, had there been no promise of coverage. In a word, it is theater.

Eden Pastora was considered a charismatic leader. He is flamboyant and bombastic, in the *macho latino* tradition. He had a mistress who has testified, on public television, that she was a spy for the Sandinistas for the entire period of her two-year association with Pastora. Did he know? Did he care? One suspects yes, and no. One suspects that Pastora spent a lot of time with a foot in two opposing camps. A suspicion like that could lower the morale of the troops.

While Pastora was generally to be found in comfortable digs in San Jose, the capital of Costa Rica, he maintained a "jungle camp" on the Nicaraguan side of the boundary river at a spot called La Penca. It could not have been a secret from the Sandinistas, but they left it alone.

When Pastora wished to issue pronouncements, it was necessary for the global press corps to follow him, by road and river, to this particular stage set, where he would appear in guerrilla garb and the journalists would all do their professional best to convince the world he always lived this way.

Tony Avirgan had *not* been invited to the press conference; Orion Pastora, a brother and a genuine anti-Communist, pointedly had failed to extend an invitation to a man whose reputation preceded him. But Tony, by offering rides to others, went along anyway.

What happened at La Penca was not theater. It was hideously real. A very substantial bomb was detonated amid the journalists, and great carnage resulted. Pastora, the presumed target, sustained a leg injury; a total of eight people were killed outright, or died in due time, and sixteen others were injured.

They were located hours away from any medical assistance. Pastora's first move was to grab the best boat and flee with the only doctor present. Well, who knows, it could have been an attack. Perhaps preserving his hide for the Cause was far more important than rallying his troops, or doing anything whatsoever for the casualties.

The result was a leaderless milling-about in the darkness, while many suffered and some died. Linda Frazier, an American journalist, had both lower legs blown off and bled to death in the mud; no one seemed to have heard of a tourniquet.

Tony Avirgan was undoubtedly shocked and gore-spattered, but his actual injuries proved to be quite minor. Which is to say, he had an awful-looking, doubtless painful, but still firmly attached middle finger on his left hand, contemplation of which seems to have absorbed his full attention. He does not report that he even attempted to give assistance to any of the more seriously injured present.

Avirgan and Honey fault the U.S. Embassy for not immediately wafting them off by magic carpet. It was a dark, rainy, foggy night without anything resembling an airstrip or even a helicopter landing-site nearby, and the magic carpets were located, in any case, in Panama. The only way out was the same as the way in—by tedious boat trip upriver, followed by hours of jouncing over bad roads.

The nature of Tony Avirgan's wounds have been variously presented. The doctor who attended him at the hospital in San Jose stated that he had "cuts on his hands." Photographs show him gore-spattered, but that was other people's gore. U.S. Ambassador Curtin Winsor recalls Avirgan as among the least injured—but the biggest crybaby present.

"Shrapnel wounds, burns, and a mangled hand" sounded better, when Tony and Martha were writing La Penca. A year after that, when trying for multi-million dollar damages, Sheehan upgraded matters in legal papers to "grievous bodily injury" and "serious physical injuries to his person."

Let us move on to Leslie Cockburn as she puts the family expertise to work in her book, Out of Control. (Her Communist father-in-law was famous for his overnight, to-order atrocity stories.) Tony "survived" but with "a mangled hand, severe burns, and 'a big hole ripped out of my side,' " she quotes the victim saying.

Not good enough. By February, 1987, Sheehan told an audience of the faithful, gullible, and credulous, "He [Avirgan] had been devastated by the bomb. It tore out a portion of his side, had burnt one whole arm and his hand, and blown shrapnel into his face and chest. He was in critical condition and was flown out by helicopter to the hospital and later to the United States, where he underwent months of plastic surgery."

By this time, if you project a trend, poor Tony is probably a torso in a basket, with his head under a bag to spare the public. The fact is, the entire description is moonshine.

In a telephone interview on August 4, 1989, the author asked Tony's mother Fran, who normally resides with the couple and their children in Costa Rica, about her son's injuries. At first she could not understand why anyone would be concerned. "He's fine," she said, although there was just a little something wrong with the middle finger of his left hand.

As for published descriptions of Tony's wounds, Fran Avirgan merely commented, "Well, you know how Mr. Sheehan likes to exaggerate." Oddly enough, they all forgot to claim a hearing impairment.

Martha Honey, when she reached Tony's bedside, was swift to deal out blame and issue demands for immediate medical evacuation. There was a delay because, well, there was some suspicion that Tony himself might have placed the bomb. After all, the Sandinistas had reason to try to kill Pastora, Tony had pushed his way into the press conference, and he was among the least hurt. He was, therefore a prime suspect to some in Costa Rica.

Ambassador Winsor, possibly to quiet Honey's nonstop clamor, facilitated the couple's departure by Learjet laid on by ABC News, although the Costa Ricans wanted to ask Tony a few questions first. The Ambassador later stated that the "main concern" of the pair "was to leave Costa Rica to avoid being involved in the government investigation of the La Penca bombing." Yet Avirgan grumbles that Ambassador Winsor suspected that he was "a communist," and says others thought he might "have ties to ETA," the Basque terrorist organization, some of whose members, displaced from their homeland in northern Spain, had taken their talents to Central America.

Avirgan makes no mention, however, of the further suspicion in Costa Rican political circles that he had something to do with the murder of Dr. Hugo Spadafora, foe of Panama's dictator, Manuel Noriega. Although in hiding, Spadafora had reluctantly granted an interview to Avirgan and Honey. The next day, his headless body turned up in a mail sack, and time had been taken for torture prior to his killing. The suspicion lingered that his hiding-place had been revealed by journalists. Which ones? Who knows.

La Penca: The Book

As for the bombing at La Penca, whodunit? Any mystery buff looks for motive, means, and opportunity. One problem is that motives abounded—Pastora had, over the years, provided all of his patrons with "motive"—and one could not even be sure all of his patrons had been identified.

The Sandinistas were obvious suspects, and many believed Pastora had worn out his welcome with the Central Intelligence Agency as well. Possibly other contras thought little of a leader who contentedly shared his bed with a Sandinista spy. The government of Muammar Qaddafi was mentioned, since Qaddafi had reportedly advanced Pastora a few million dollars, and regarded the return on his investment as unsatisfactory. And there were the Basques . . .

It seems *outré* but, in Central America today, there is sometimes an unholy alliance between Marxist Basque Jesuit priests and homeless Basque terrorists. They share a common frustrated nationalism. Now that the French have ceased to turn a blind eye upon the *etarras* fleeing the consequences of their actions in Spain, many have become "homeless persons," and the Soviets are often their only remaining patrons. In any case, a Central America in turmoil offers employment opportunities for Basques on the run.

There is need here for an aside—a note as to source. The Christic Institute publishes *Brought to Light,* a nine-dollar comic book—for that price, it is called "a graphic docudrama album," but we will call it Christic Comix. It contains the Christic version of events, and is a very good way to enter into their mindset; the author has found it a useful source indeed. One half of the comic book is a truly lurid attack upon the CIA and present-day America, while the other half depicts the adventures of Avirgan and Honey. There is a brief center section done by a cartoonist who has made a living "drug-peddling" via his creation, "The Fabulous Furry Freak Brothers." Hypocrisy, anyone?

Christic Comix is at particular pains to ridicule the Basque possibility. They point to a warning issued "in mid-1983" about Basque terrorists in Central America, dismiss it as CIA nonsense, and then conclude that it had been planted "for a reason," evidently to set the stage—a year in advance?—for what has to be the world's most glacially-paced assassination scheme.

Back to the bombing at La Penca.

Motives abounded. As for means, there were plenty of weapons about.

And opportunity? It would seem likely that Pastora was better-guarded when venturing into Nicaragua than he was when in San Jose. For an assassin, the problem of a getaway from La Penca appears daunting.

It is quite likely, although by no means proven, that the actual assassin— the man who carried, planted, and detonated the bomb—is the man pictured, but not really identified, in coverage of the event. This was a man using a Danish passport in the name of Per Anker Hansen, and purporting to be a journalist for a news organization in Europe which no one had ever heard of. "Hansen" attached himself to a Swedish journalist, Peter Torbjornson, who says he accepted the story that "Hansen" had been raised in Venezuela, and therefore spoke Spanish like a native, but not a word of Danish.

The passport was variously reported as being lost by, or stolen from, a "student," or a "leftist railway worker" in Denmark way back in December, 1980. It also could have been donated to the Cause. Christic Comix says "Hansen" used it to go to Panama and rent "a luxury high-rise apartment" more than a year later, in 1982. (And then in 1983 they planted the Basque rumor, and in the middle of 1984 they got around to the bomb attack . . .)

The phony "Hansen" was among the group of journalists being brought, via motorized dugouts, to the picturesque jungle camp on the riverbank, in full view of any passing Sandinista patrols. "Hansen" was conveniently out of the building when the bomb detonated, but made no effort to get away; he calmly waited out the night and the lengthy, miserable evacuation. In San Jose, he lingered in the hospital awhile with minor injuries, gave an interview to another journalist, went to his hotel, checked out—and totally disappeared.

Omitted from consideration, in *La Penca,* is Torbjornson, the fellow who traveled with "Hansen" for weeks, and allegedly accepted him as a fellow Scandinavian. Torbjornson, too, was virtually uninjured and also left Costa Rica as soon as possible. He had the greatest contact with "Hansen," and should have been the person most likely to spot him as a phony. Yet he seems never to have been considered suspicious by Avirgan and Honey.

The Newspaper Guild—a famous old lefty (but mainstream) outfit—the Committee to Protect Journalists, starring David Marash, a Washington-area TV newscaster, and a Norwegian journalists' union, are said to have provided the money which allowed Martha Honey to roam the earth in search of the "Hansen" chimera.

One can see this, on a gut level, as the effort of one tough mama to nail whoever gave her Tony a bad experience. But, with these two, everything exists in an ideological wash. It was a foregone conclusion that this pair would never print a book blaming the left, in any of its many guises, regardless of what they discovered.

Compared to later, smoothed-out versions showing the touch of a master Irish story-teller, the booklet *La Penca* comes across as a crude but more honest effort. Because, essentially, Avirgan and Honey came up empty on "Hansen." It wasn't for want of the opportunity to chase down possibilities. A hot suspect of the desired ideological hue was pursued all the way to Uruguay, but proved to be *way* off as to height.

Christic Institute attorney Sheehan would have found a cure for that— such as failing to mention it. That is what we mean by crude but more honest.

In *La Penca*, "Hansen" becomes "Amac Galil" on the flimsiest of grounds, if indeed grounds exist at all. That is, one must first believe in the Christic story of David.

David, with no last name, was the "source" of all the information which Avirgan and Honey were lacking. It was *so* fortunate! And, then, as the story goes, he was kidnapped, tortured, murdered, and buried on John Hull's farm. It was *so* unfortunate . . . John Hull, an American farmer in Costa Rica, was destined for rough handling by Avirgan, Honey and the Christics.

We must all try to picture this; the Christics swear to it. A stranger walks into a bar on March 29, 1985—you will need the date—approaches a patron he never saw before in his life, and *in ten minutes,* vouchsafes to him the following carload of inside information:

That he is part of a "a right-wing terrorist ring operating in Central America," which is about to dynamite the U.S. Embassy. He is an anti-Sandinista who finds his companions "much more evil." His fellow terrorists consist of "anti-Sandinista Nicaraguans, Costa Ricans, Cuban exiles and North Americans." They form a sort of dirty tricks unit within the FDN. They have ties with anti-Castro extremist groups such as Alpha 66, Omega 7, and Brigade 2506. They also have ties to the CIA. They operate from safe houses and contra camps in Honduras, Costa Rica, Panama, Nicaragua, and Miami. He mentioned they are based on a farm owned by John Hull . . . David outlined the group's mission as threefold: to eliminate Eden Pastora from the southern front so that the FDN can move in; to provoke conflict between Nicaragua and its neighbors, and to provoke direct U.S. military action against Nicaragua. But they also traffic in cocaine, marijuana, and arms. They did the assassination at La Penca, and although it failed, the group is still intact and prepared to commit further atrocities, even as we speak.

We are to believe that Carlos Rojas Chinchilla, the bar patron, kept this all straight in his head until April 25, 1985, four weeks later, when he decided to download the lot onto one Julia Meeks, who told her employers, Avirgan and Honey, who then announce, "the broad outline we already had assembled of an FDN/Cuban/CIA terrorist ring fit with the information he told us." As chance would have it.

So they asked Carlos to talk to "David" again. Carlos evidently had no trouble in complying, and came back to relay the following:

> The bomber who posed as a Danish photojournalist named "Per Anker Hansen" is, in reality, a Libyan who calls himself Amac Galil. He was hired in Chile by two FDN [contra] officials and a North American CIA agent who poses as a journalist. David said that Galil is highly professional and, as a Libyan, was considered ideal for the job. If he were killed, captured, or otherwise identified, it was reasoned, it would be assumed he was working for Col. Muammar Qaddafi.

"While no other source [than David] has named Galil, and we know nothing more about him, he appears plausible. . ." quoth our journalistic team. Thus is born Amac Galil! He was soon to develop an appropriate accent.

David said $50,000 was passed from the CIA through the FDN for expenses in the bombing operation. [David was standing right there and they let him count it? Or the package had "$50,000" marked on it? Or he could tell at a glance? Or the bad guys announced to the foot-soldier standing by, "This is fifty thousand yankee-dollars for expenses in the bombing operation?" Give us all a break!]

"David" told Carlos, on July 17, that "Amac Galil and a hit team were due in Costa Rica within a few days to begin their terrorist attacks." But nothing happened.

So here we have the sum total of evidence as to one "Amac Galil." Flimsy, indeed, but the Christics believe in him.

And then, in true comic-book style, Carlos and David are kidnapped, taken to the bad guys' headquarters, overhear comments incriminating John Hull, overpower their guards and flee under a hail of bullets, travel for days, and finally reach safety. But alas, we have already heard what allegedly happened later to David. There goes the prize witness. What a pity that his stories cannot be confirmed, but you see how utterly ruthless these villains are . . .

The booklet *La Penca* first circulated in Spanish translation in Costa Rica, starting in September, 1985. Its purposes were to blame the contras, John Hull, and the CIA for the bombing. John Hull sued for libel as soon as he read the thing, meaning about October, 1985. The case did not reach court until mid-May of 1986, by which time Avirgan and Honey had been linked up with the Christics for about five months. Hull, anticipating little problem, used an inexperienced local lawyer—and lost the case.

David had been identified from his contra ID card as Jarald David Morero Cardoncillo. The David shown in Christic Comix is that David. There must have been a little slip-up somewhere, a scheduling glitch, because his tortured body never showed up on Hull's farm. His live body showed up, however, and said it had never heard of these people, and never said these things.

But if you think evidence counts for much, with the legal terrorists, think again.

CHAPTER THREE

WHO ARE THE CHRISTICS?

Rev. William J. Davis, S.J.

July 24–25, 1975, in New York City—"A People's Salute to Cuba . . . As we celebrate this 22nd anniversary of the Moncada assault that sparked the victorious Cuban revolution, I wish to add my name to the thousands [sending] fraternal greetings . . ."

The "Moncada assault" was Fidel Castro's attack on a Cuban army barracks in 1953. Journalist Georgie Anne Geyer knows it as "a crazy, sacrificial attack."

"These innocent young people," she told a conference in January, 1989, "going to a sure death, and Fidel not caring at all, because he's making his point in history . . ."

Often called a "failed" attack, it was only a failure for Castro's followers; it was a prime career move for Fidel.

So we find, signing up to congratulate Fidel, "Communist Party, USA . . . George W. Crockett, Jr. [currently Chairman of the House Subcommittee on Western Hemisphere Affairs] . . . Angela Davis, Communist Party, USA . . . William S. (sic) Davis, S.J., Office of Social Ministries, Jesuit Conference . . ."

The lengthy list consisted of the hard core of the American Communist Party, plus an instructive array of front-groups, as of mid-1975. By his own choice, we find Davis in this rather special company.

Does this make Father Davis a Communist? Well, it opens the question to examination, and it certainly marks him as a "fellow traveler," an expression invented by the Communists to be applied to their allies.

Informal inquiries in Rome produce the report that Davis was suspended from the priesthood about five years ago, and remains so. A query to his superiors in the Oregon Province produced total evasion. Certainly, Father Davis does not appear to have any priestly duties.

Father Davis—just call him "Bill," or even "Billy," if you're part of the "movement"—has worn his politics on his sleeve for at least fourteen years, possibly sixteen, perhaps even more. It would appear that he has gone too far.

William J. Davis was born in an all-American spot—Havre, Montana—on July 20, 1934. This makes him a greybeard among the Christic tribe. He entered the Jesuit order in September, 1952 and was ordained as a Jesuit priest in June, 1965.

He is a "liberation theology" acolyte, and says in certain publications that he has traveled in Central America since about 1967. This may well have brought him into contact with Cesar Jerez, a Guatemalan Communist and Jesuit. Yes, priests can become Communists, and Communists can become priests. Jerez was actively involved with Marxists in San Salvador in 1970.

In 1973, Cesar Jerez was invited to address a Jesuit symposium in Boston, also attended by Father Davis. There, Jerez tried to whip up a more radical Marxist spirit among American Jesuit priests, telling them that "the function of Jesuits in the Third World is to create conflict. We are the only powerful group in the world today to do it."

One may wonder when the Communists dropped out of the game!

Probably in 1974, Davis went to Chile to "investigate" the death of an American who became the subject of a Communist "docudrama." Charles Horman was killed in the wake of the very popular military coup which relieved Chile of the incubus of Salvador Allende and his "foreign legion" of Communist supporters.

Horman's father was encouraged by Cora Weiss' husband, Peter Weiss, to sue then-Secretary of State Henry Kissinger and then-Ambassador Nathaniel Davis for his son's death. (The suit was dismissed "without prejudice" in 1981.) Peter Weiss sat astride the Rubin Fund money, financing William Kunstler's activities as the legal "top gun" of the hard left.

The lawsuit was followed by a book, and then a movie. The Greek left-wing film producer, Constantin Costa-Gavras, who specialized in anti-establishment films like *Z* and *State of Siege,* came up with *Missing,* with the assistance of the widow of Communist "'agent of influence'' Orlando Letelier, a former Chilean diplomat.

Letelier's activities on behalf of the Cubans were exposed when he was killed by a bomb in the middle of Washington, and his briefcase came into the hands of the Federal Bureau of Investigation.

Ambassador Davis and the Embassy's former military attache then sued for libel, but once again, the judicial system favored their attackers. As it was explained in legal journals, the defendant publishers and film distributors had the case moved from the Eastern District of Virginia, where the trial might be speedy, and there were many military personnel around who might become jurors, to the Southern District of Manhattan, where everyone might die of old age before the court got around to the case, and the media have tremendous clout.

Father William Davis became head of the Jesuit Office of Social Ministry (singular, as per telephone directory listing, but just as often written ''Ministries'') early in 1975. Some time during that year, Daniel Sheehan came aboard as counsel. How Davis and Sheehan found each other is not known.

Daniel Sheehan

"Now comes,'' in the jargon of the law, Daniel Sheehan. He was born in upstate New York in 1945, and seems to have led the life of a normal Irish Catholic boy all the way through high school.

According to James Traub's article in *Mother Jones,* he wanted to be an astronaut, but was aced out of a spot at the Air Force Academy by a politician's son—"Sheehan's first experience with political injustice,'' according to Traub.

His next stop was Northeastern University, in Boston, where he signed up for "the elite corps of ROTC, training to be a Green Beret,'' but they freaked him out with the one about removing heads with piano wire. (A real live Green Beret says it works, too, although all that's wanted is a silent death, and a full neck-ectomy is hardly necessary for that.)

So saying, Sheehan found Harvard more to his liking. Traub again: "Everyone was popping magic mushrooms and studying Zen.'' And womb-clinging, and ducking the draft, let us not forget.

Sheehan graduated from Harvard Law in 1970 and walked into a big New York law firm, as one would expect. But his heart was in *pro bono* leftist ambulance-chasing.

What really turned him on was defending "Black Panthers accused of a plot to blow up Macy's,'' according to Richard Rashke, author of a book about the Karen Silkwood case which meets with the approval of Sheehan. Sheehan was also on the edge of the Pentagon Papers case, although in his own account of things, he is never on the fringe of anything, but always the star.

The law firm's complaint was that Sheehan was so absorbed in his unpaid work for the left that he would not keep his mind on any of the paying jobs. When he was let go, Sheehan claimed that Alger Hiss—role model and hero?—had been fired from that firm for the same reason.

The law firm says no, Danny Sheehan says yes. The wish, in Sheehan's case, is so very often father to the fact. . .

A stint with F. Lee Bailey looks great on a resume, but did not work out too well in reality. Bailey loved a legal slugfest, but was insufficiently ideological for Sheehan's taste. They soon parted company.

At some point, Sheehan went back to school to study "social ethics." These were exciting times for ethics, and "liberation theology" also allowed for novel interpretations of God's will. One cannot obtain clarification relative to these little points, because of Christic standing orders prohibiting the conveyance of any information whatsoever to the author about key personalities in the Christic organization. Is this not a strange posture for a tax-free organization dedicated to public policy issues to take?

When the ACLU offered Sheehan the opportunity to defend American Indian Movement (AIM) strongarm man Russell Means, he mounted up and rode West. The AIM toughs who descended as a small army upon the Oglala Sioux Reservation in South Dakota, first in a dry run in 1972, then for real in 1973, had police "pedigrees" a yard long, and were armed with a generous variety of weapons—but posed for the cameras with Soviet AK-47s. They were armed felons, a no-no under the liberals' own favorite Gun Control Act of 1968, and they killed people at Wounded Knee, but they were met with vast indulgence by leftist church and media representatives.

The author "made the scene" at Wounded Knee in 1973 and is quite familiar with the cast and plot. Crimes committed by Russell Means and his fifty carloads of hoodlums included thievery and robbery, assault and battery, kidnapping, cattle rustling, rioting, arson, and illegal possession of firearms. The list could go on, because it *was* a ten-week occupation by a lawless horde. Moscow's *New Times* played it big, and Means sent back to Moscow fraternal greetings and heartfelt gratitude.

To the author's knowledge, no one was ever convicted of burning alive

Leo Wilcox on March 25, 1973, but AIM's Leonard Peltier was eventually convicted of killing two FBI agents. Naturally, Peltier remains a "political prisoner" visited by Soviet officials solicitous of his fate.

The Wounded Knee episode is a fine example of radical church and media collaboration in support of domestic "revolution." The National and World Councils of Churches were up to their armpits in the support and protection of the invaders. This alliance of criminals, church radicals, the mass media, and the Communists created docudrama in the round. Very instructive.

It should be noted that these church bodies turn a blind eye to KGB officers who present themselves as officials of Soviet religious groups.

Sheehan was hired by Father Davis as counsel for the Jesuit Office of Social Ministry in 1975. "By then," writes Traub, "he was a veteran agitator and public-interest lawyer." Sheehan's notion of the public interest should be clear enough.

It is said that Sheehan considered becoming a Jesuit. Had Sheehan been serious, and started down the same path as Davis in 1975, he would have been kept out of mischief until 1988. Instead, the Davis-Sheehan team soon busied itself with the legal defense of the radical brother-priests, the Berrigans, and Dick Gregory, the black comedian who had ceased to be funny. This group had demonstrated on the White House lawn because the amnesty for "draft evaders and deserters" was not sweeping enough for their tastes. Sheehan got them off. One of the Berrigans then told Sheehan that the National Organization of Women needed a free lawyer of his ideological orientation.

The Karen Silkwood Case

Books have been written about the Silkwood case—and at least one more ought to be. It is important to us here because it brought together Sheehan and his future wife, Sara Nelson, converted Father Davis into a gumshoe and process-server, and reveals the *modus operandi* of those who eventually formed the Christic Institute.

Karen Silkwood has been the subject of the proverbial major motion picture, starring Meryl Streep, the actress who helped to touch off a national hysteria about apples, early in 1989. In *Silkwood,* we can see "docudrama" as *dezinformatsiya,* or disinformation, American style.

The word "docudrama" is of recent confection, a clever combination of "documentary" and drama, which is to say, of fact and fiction. In the public subconscious, there is something mysterious and impressive about the word "document." It conjures up the image of ancient script on vellum, of proclamations bearing waxen seals—or, at the very least, of legal verbiage on top-of-the-line bond paper.

Trading on the weightiness of the word "document," we are invited to believe that movie or television scriptwriters have labored long and hard in dusty archives. But your run-of-Hollywood scriptwriter would not be found dead in an archive. The "documents," where they exist at all, are more likely the handouts of contending parties. They are not allowed to stand in the way of either drama or the party line. The drama is necessary in order to keep the attention of the target audience, while the party line is hammered home.

The book by Richard Rashke, *The Killing of Karen Silkwood,* (note the presumption of homicide) provides much background on the future leading lights of the Christic Institute. This was a needed service, in view of the refusal of the Christics to provide the author with any factual information whatsoever.

Rashke worked for the *National Catholic Reporter,* and was an early fan of Davis, Sheehan, and Nelson. Nonetheless, the book is a useful source on the Silkwood case, even though it presents the version the Christics consider most favorable to their cause, which is why they sell it.

We must also thank Nick Thimmesch for the debunking of *Silkwood,* which appeared in the *Washington Post,* December 11, 1983. He debunks the "docudrama" version of her death—she is driving along a lonely road with "the documents" when "an ominous vehicle comes up from behind; there is a blinding reflection of its headlights in her rear-view mirror, and then a full-screen whiteout, with Silkwood hurtled to a martyr's death."

As Thimmesch points out, there were no "documents" to be found, nor any evidence of another vehicle. On the other hand, our heroine was so loaded with Quaaludes that the best face her partisans could place upon it was that she had probably built up an unusual tolerance for them. She also had a record of running off roads.

Karen Silkwood was a divorced mother of three whose husband had custody of the children. She had a job at the Kerr-McGee plutonium plant in Crescent, Oklahoma. The film fudges her odd indifference to her children, but, more likely in deference to the values of the National Organization of Women than to standard propaganda practice, it does not fudge her lifestyle. She was sexually promiscuous, smoked like a chimney—both tobacco and marijuana—and drank, but evidently not to excess.

The film does not reveal her addiction to uppers and downers, nor her attempted suicide by drug overdose in 1973. Silkwood was hooked on 'ludes until her death in November, 1974.

After an unsuccessful strike at the Kerr-McGee plant in the fall of 1972, the Oil, Chemical, and Atomic Workers' Union was inactive there until late in 1974. Karen Silkwood, however, became interested in union activity. A visit to Washington and patronization by union bigwigs filled her with dreams of a life outside Crescent, Oklahoma.

The union was pursuing a twin strategy. The first one was to scare the workers silly with the message that they were probably going to get cancer in thirty or forty years. "Did the company tell you that?" Consider—you don't have to work at Kerr-McGee in order to get cancer in thirty or forty years.

The second strategy was to use Karen Silkwood to substantiate a claim that Kerr-McGee was selling the government defective fuel rods. (Since the fuel rods were also inspected by the recipient, and since a certain small percentage were routinely rejected, this would not seem to be any big deal.)

She assured a union official, Steve Wodka, that she would deliver the proof, and he set up a meeting with a *New York Times* reporter for her. She could see her name in lights, and perhaps fancied herself being carried from the banks of the Cimarron to the big city of Washington by a new, powerful lover. At the very least, she could imagine herself a rising star in the union. So this assignment was important to her.

The Rashke book would have us believe that Karen Silkwood was an intellectual-in-the-rough. This is not a point pursued in the film. She had a high-school education, and was a lab worker in a plutonium plant—evidently a competent one, when she was doing the job she was paid to do. But a little knowledge can be a dangerous thing. She may even have contaminated herself with plutonium deliberately, to make a point—and then panicked at the thought that she might have overdone it!

In October of 1974, she had asked what would happen if she swallowed a plutonium pellet, and was told, nothing much. Plutonium is chiefly a danger to lung tissue. Also in October, she inquired about her "hot" urine samples before anyone at the plant had tested them. How she happened to know that they would prove "hot" has never been explained.

Early in November, 1974, a peculiar pattern of contamination came to light. It is most logically explained by the assumption that Silkwood was herself responsible. An *insoluble* plutonium showed up in her urine—meaning that it was impossible for it to have passed through her system—and this contaminant was present only in urine samples brought from home, never in samples taken under supervision at the plant.

When Silkwood learned that Kerr-McGee was sending around a crew to check out her home for radioactivity, she called to warn her friend to stay away from the kitchen and bathroom. Too late—her friend had a temporarily radioactive bottom from the toilet seat. As the story developed, it seems that Silkwood had placed a bologna sandwich on the toilet while dibbling with her urine sample, and then placed the sandwich in the refrigerator. The purpose of the exercise, as far as anyone can imagine, must have been to discredit Kerr-McGee on the safety issue.

Silkwood does appear to have panicked, thinking that the radiation might have doomed her, but a trip to Los Alamos for a very expensive examination—paid for, naturally, by the company—assured her to the contrary.

Nevertheless, Karen Silkwood was one strung-out individual on the eve of her death. She had been under a strain, trying to locate and sneak out the "documents" she had promised Steve Wodka. The business with the urine samples had given her a considerable scare, she was popping Quaaludes, and had lost about twenty pounds she could ill afford, during the past month.

With or without "the documents," Karen Silkwood ran off the road and died on the night of November 13, 1974.

Enter Sara Nelson

Although the union certainly wanted to make hay of Silkwood's death, no one on the scene in Oklahoma saw anything sinister or conspiratorial about it. The union and its media allies raised as much dust as they could, drawing in the Federal Bureau of Investigation, calling in Congressional markers, but despite their best efforts, the case was closed early in 1975.

At that time Sara Nelson, then 32, was in Washington as national director of the Labor Task Force of the National Organization of Women. She was militantly pro-union and also a power in the NOW faction yelling, "Out of the mainstream, into the revolution!"—the slogan they would carry to the floor of the 1976 NOW convention in Philadelphia.

When the Silkwood case was brought to her attention, Sara Nelson decided to adopt it as her Cause. The "issue" would be the brave little girl going up against the bad men of the big evil corporation, and being cut down in the prime of her life. The union gladly handed off the Silkwood case to NOW. By July 20, 1975, Rashke writes, the strategy was worked out. NOW called an "action alert" for August 26, with the slogan "Stop Violence Against Women NOW." A media and lobbying campaign was part of the package. "Who Killed Karen Silkwood?" posters appeared like magic. You can still see one in the Christic Institute's reception area.

In the usual absence of information from the Christics, we can only say that Sara Nelson was probably born in 1943, and is from North Dakota.

She is a graduate of the University of California at Berkeley, probably about 1965 or so; she worked for Community Access Television of California, then became "co-director of and producer for American Documentary Films, Inc., of New York and San Francisco." The latter outfit is still in the propaganda business, since its "documentaries," according to current executive producer Marc Weiss, make "no apologies for advocacy."

If yelling and screaming can make it so, Sara Nelson can make it so. The Silkwood episode was reopened, Nelson was on it full-time, and she needed a "movement" lawyer. One of the Berrigans directed Sara Nelson's attention to the Jesuit Office of Social Ministry, thus bringing Davis, Sheehan, and Nelson together.

Davis remained in charge of the Office of Social Ministry until some time in 1977, but the situation was becoming increasingly distasteful to the broader Jesuit community. For one thing, according to Rashke, the other Jesuits "had taken a strong dislike" to Sheehan, "whom they considered disrespectful and pushy."

Not mentioned in the Rashke book, but possibly a factor, may have been Davis' public sponsorship, with the Communist Party, of the Moncada Barracks anniversary. There may have been more to that association, known to the Jesuits but kept quiet.

Yet another contributing element of unease must have been the hot-and-cold-running pro-abortion females from the National Organization of Women, under foot at all hours of the day and night. The "work" of the Office of Social Ministry was becoming a one-note threnody having very little to do with the Church.

Rendered temporarily homeless, Davis, Sheehan, and Nelson were "taken in," in 1977, by Jesuit Father William Callahan, who found he could afford to pay them each $700 a month out of his Quixote Center budget.

But greater things were just around the corner for Quixote Center. Father Cesar Jerez—the Guatemalan Communist Jesuit—had moved onward and upward in his career. In 1976, he became Jesuit Provincial for Central America, and in 1977, he maneuvered the selection of Oscar Romero as

Archbishop of San Salvador. In 1978, Jerez came to Washington, D.C., to oversee the creation of the Religious Task Force on Central America. This became an umbrella organization for three Catholic groups in the capital—Jesuit Missions, the Center for Concern—and Quixote Center. The latter, in turn, spawned Quest for Peace. At last report, early in 1989, Quest would claim to have dispatched over $115 million worth of goods to the *comandantes* in Nicaragua. Thus, there is no question as to the origin, orientation, and support of both Quixote and Quest.

The extensive activity of Sheehan and Davis in Oklahoma, Texas, Tennessee, and other states, and the even more extensive activities of their mysterious investigator, Bill Taylor, who had anonymous sources everywhere (a recurrent feature of Sheehan investigations) was not financed by $700 a month from Quixote Center.

Sara Nelson's *forte* is fund-raising and organization. She was able to draw upon some notable left-wing sources, such as the National Emergency Civil Liberties Foundation and the Stern Fund. ("Ah, the Old Left," sighed one intelligence specialist.) These sources of Red gold kicked in to the obscure Catholic Quixote Center when the Nelson-Sheehan-Davis trio climbed aboard.

The Communists have a durable campaign to deny the United States the benefit of nuclear *anything,* and will encourage any effort to reduce the public to a state of irrational hysteria. The late 1970s were a period of intense agitation, which has resulted in the near-strangulation of the nuclear power industry.

Nelson's fund-raising brought the trio into contact with rocker Jackson Browne, with whom she formed a group of anti-nuke musicians, perfect peddlers of irrational hysteria. Also at this time a relationship developed with David Fenton, their future publicist, and with reliable money-cows like Maryanne Mott and Max and Anna Levinson.

The Silkwood Trial

The Silkwood trial was not Sheehan's conspiracy extravaganza, a confection based upon anonymous informants and really extended speculation. That was thrown out of court. Rather it was Gerry Spence's negligence trial.

Spence was brought in by Sheehan, who knew he could not handle the court case. Spence, in his own book, *Gunning for Justice,* gives us his impression of Sheehan:

What followed was a torrent of words, a huge passel of information

. . . about the FBI, the CIA, NSA, LEIU—there were super-computers and conspiracies dating back to Bobby Kennedy's attorney generalship. Silkwood had been bugged, followed, contaminated, harassed, and maybe murdered and "they" were responsible. . .

"Danny Sheehan has a five-minute, fifteen-minute, thirty-minute, a two-hour, and an all-night version of the Silkwood case . . . I later learned that Sara Nelson had a mystical insight that I was the right man [for the case].

". . . Sheehan didn't seem so much lawyer as politician. He had to keep his own troops motivated to keep the cause alive, to gather up the funds necessary to support the cause. . .

"[There were] certain mystical powers, a connectedness, an instinctive knowledge of things Sheehan claimed to possess. You'd better not ask, or he'd launch into an excruciatingly convoluted intellectual discussion of the metaphysical that left one exhausted and frustrated. . .

"He terrorized his opponents. They seethed and suffered and cried in outrage, but they were unable to divert him or reason with him. . .

"Besides, he was the ultimate earth authority, plugged in as he was to the ultimate cosmic authority. I thought he was either a saint or a charlatan, but I always left room for the proposition that he had a direct line into those mysterious places that he claimed to know."

Lawyer Spence knew that Sara Nelson controlled the purse-strings. He bemoans the "hundreds of thousands of dollars"—forget those $700-a-month stipends—expended in pursuit of mystical hunches, and he notes the manner in which he was stiffed for $25,000 by Nelson.

When it comes to the trial, Spence does not tell us what Sheehan's specific contribution to his own case against Kerr-McGee may have been, but we suspect it included rounding up anti-nukes John Gofman and Karl Morgan, who were already reliable workhorses on the witness stand.

Spence had to prove that Kerr-McGee's plutonium had done "physical injury" to Karen Silkwood. She had an estimated 8 nanocuries (billionths of a curie) of plutonium in her lungs, with a margin of error of 300%, meaning anywhere from 2.7 to 24 nanocuries. The margin of error was that large because the quantity was so minute that it could hardly be measured.

The jury was assured by expert witness John Gofman that she was "married to cancer" from the moment of contamination onward. Gofman knew, at the time, of the 25 Manhattan Project workers who had accidentally received doses of up to 230 nanocuries back in 1944–45. He knew they were all still alive in 1979, 35 years later, and not one of them had *any* form of internal cancer (though some had moles!).

Oh, but they had "a myriad of frightening health problems—blindness, high blood pressure, heart attacks, tooth loss, respiratory ailments, mouth tumors, thyroid nodules. . ." High blood pressure? Tooth loss? Colds? Mouth tumors from smoking?? All of us should know no greater terrors, thirty-five years down the road!

Funny thing—by 1989, when the average age must have been close to 70, there was *still* no lung cancer, although two men had died of other causes. The surviving 23 men constitute the IPPu Club, meaning I Pee Plutonium. They meet annually, and everyone is very interested in their health. They may be proving that plutonium is *good* for you. There is, in fact, the phenomenon known as hormesis; at times, a little of a bad thing can do you good.

In the Los Alamos Plutonium Workers Study of 224 workers who had been exposed to 10 nanocuries or more, normal mortality rates projected 62 deaths in that group, 11 from cancer. But there had been only 33 deaths (Spence does not tell us how many from cancer).

But Spence *won* the case on the basis of hysteria-mongering which he himself quite proudly quotes from his opening statement. He told the jury, "The evidence will be that [Silkwood] would actually, *absolutely have died* from this horrid radiation from plutonium, from the willful and wanton conduct of Kerr-McGee." The facts do not support that conclusion, but there was plenty more out of Spence in this rabble-rousing vein.

Just as an aside, by 1984, Gofman and Morgan had been making a good living for many years as "professional anti-nuclear witnesses," appearing in close to four dozen trials along the lines of the Silkwood case. But in November, 1984, Judge Patrick Kelly of the U.S. District Court in Kansas finally threw out their ever more specious arguments. He pointed out that, by their standards, "a person in Kansas would have a tort duty to label every bucketful of dirt he owned, [and] a Kansas town would be required to label every 600 gallons of public water."

By Gofman's standards, another physicist once noted, our own bodies contain so much radioactive potassium 40 and carbon 14 that we should be dealt with as toxic waste. Morgan and Gofman are still carrying the can for the Christics. In October 1989, the Christics used them in their attempt to halt deployment of the Galileo space probe. Fortunately, they failed.

Spence tells us he was uneasy about the effect which the coterie of glassy-eyed, freaky-looking "cause people" were having on public opinion. He tells us that he blew up and cussed out Sara Nelson when she unlimbered her bullhorn for a premature victory rally outside the jury room, while the jury was still deliberating.

"The jury," Spence wrote, "trusted me. I was the Silkwood case, not what they might see as a bunch of women's libbers, hippies, wild-eyed anti-nukes." Not, he says, that he was against their causes—he, too, "liked them liberated," was pro-union and anti-nuke, but these people "would surely offend one of the jurors."

"But the women hated me now. I had no 'social conscience,' no 'social sensitivity.' I was a cruel, bullying sonofabitch who didn't care about the women's cause."

Well, now, we *do* have a crafty lawyer here, one who hangs his hat in Wyoming and sports the macho image. It would do him little future good to be seen locally as a "cause" lawyer and women's libber. He doth protest too much.

Spence also found it tough to tolerate an ego at least the size of his own, meaning Danny Sheehan's. Needless to say, Spence never allowed Sheehan to set foot in "his" courtroom during the Silkwood trial.

Since Sheehan's big "conspiracy" version had been dismissed as nonsense, Spence therefore found it annoying, to put it mildly, to overhear this exchange between Sheehan and reporters, immediately after the jury brought in a verdict against Kerr-McGee.

"Well," [Sheehan] said to a reporter, "That's fifty-eight."

"Fifty-eight what?"

"Fifty-eight in a row I've won."

When it came time to appear on the *Today* show, Sheehan was the star they fawned over. Tom Brokaw "wasn't interested in me," Spence complains.

But never mind. Spence looked forward to his half of a $10.5 million settlement!

The Birth of the Christic Institute

Despite reliable leftist funding sources, the "hundreds of thousands" Gerry Spence had seen expended chasing phantoms of evil in the Silkwood case was not fully covered. They seem to have run up considerable debt, leaving Father William Callahan of the Quixote Center doubtless appalled at its weight.

For whatever reason, Sheehan, Nelson, and Davis decided to set forth on their own; they carried with them some, or all, of the debt burden. Sara Nelson was probably confident of her fund-raising abilities.

The Christic Institute, an "interfaith center for law and public policy" was set up in 1981 by Davis, and religion pervades the early pronouncements. Naturally, it applied for 501(c)(3) tax-exempt status, and received it in due time. The name was derived from Jesuit Father Pierre Teilhard de Chardin, who wrote of a "Christic force" which would unite these "like minds doing battle against evil." What Teilhard envisioned, however, was that "the Christian God on high and the Marxist God of Progress are reconciled in Christ."

This view was better-received in Moscow, where the good Father's works are on display with those of Marx and Lenin, than in the Vatican, which reacted with reserve. The barbarities of World War II and Stalinism put this theory on ice for several decades, but the "convergence" between Christianity and Marxism was revived by radical Jesuits as "liberation theology" in the early 1970s.

Early Christic "causes" were mostly anti-nuclear, with a sideline in South-bashing which would soon develop a life of its own. Income was lower in the second year than in the first.

Meanwhile, Cesar Jerez was having his troubles. The Jesuits had been allowed to drift from Rome toward Moscow, under the leadership of Father General Pedro Arrupe y Gondra. Pope John Paul I, in 1978, had prepared a speech censuring the Jesuits, just the day before his unexpected death.

However, Jerez had gained a foothold at Jesuit-run Georgetown University, and in 1980 he began overseeing the indoctrination of students sent to him in Nicaragua by "liberation theology" enthusiasts on the Georgetown faculty, such as Father Otto Hentz.

Pope John Paul II got around to a housecleaning in 1981, when he replaced the aged Father General Arrupe with a caretaker. Bad actors like Father Manuel Perez, given the choice, chose the career of a guerrilla leader in Colombia. Father Cesar Jerez was removed as Provincial for Central America in 1982, and hitched his wagon to the Sandinista star. Yet this was the very year in which he set up the Central American Historical Institute, with offices and telex terminals in Managua—and at Georgetown University in Washington. Incredibly, in 1984, Jerez was appointed a member of Georgetown University's Board of Directors. He remains in that position, as of 1989. The Christic association with the radical Jesuits of Central America is an enduring one.

We have traced the roots of the Christic Institute through the adult lives of its leading figures. The radical leftist thrust is clear from beginning to end. We need only trace it a bit further in order to bring it to 1985, when Avirgan and Honey linked up with Davis, Sheehan and Nelson to initiate the La Penca lawsuit. This was more profitable than the Silkwood case, but it remains to be seen whether it will prove as enduring in American popular mythology.

On January 12, 1982, the Christics acquired a run-down building, 1324 North Capitol Street, in one of the slum areas just thirteen blocks north of the United States Capitol Building. The transaction seems a bit unusual. The previous owner, one Maria Totaro, yielded the building to the Corporation of the Roman Catholic Clergy of Maryland, and this building was *immediately*—as the very next transfer of property registered in the District of Columbia—handed off to the Christic Institute.

The aforementioned Corporation is also known as the Maryland Province of the Society of Jesus, and as the Jesuit Fathers and Brothers of Maryland (which is the telephone listing). A query about this transaction brought a sense of caution and unease at the other end of the line. "What are the implications?" was the counter-question, before a response of any kind was extracted. Eventually, the voice allowed as how the Corporation may have owned the property at 1324 "for a couple of years." When the author said it looked more like about ten minutes, it was granted that it could have been that, too . . . Whatever the reason for caution and unease, it would appear that the arrangement was one between consenting priests. The author was reminded that this was a Jesuit *community,* an apostolic order, its purpose is to help people, Jesuits are human instruments who bring people to the love of God, Father Davis is a Jesuit, we were happy to do it for him, he did so much good in the Silkwood case. . . All right! All right!

A year later, in January of 1983, the Christics were able to acquire the adjacent building, 1322 North Capitol. This was just another seedy row house, in an area where their neighbors are such as to require that the windows be boarded up, or covered with a tight-mesh wire grill. The abundance of locks probably attests to both the neighborhood and the endemic atmosphere of paranoia.

Christic vows of poverty are fairly convincing. Father Davis was listed, in the Christics' tax return, as having had a salary of $15,000 one year— and none the next. Still, it's hard to believe that a man of 55 does not even receive any pocket money. . .

Sheehan and Nelson paid themselves $15,000 a year until recently, when they gave themselves a raise to $21,000 a year. But they live and breathe their Cause, so everything is a Cause expense. The tax return has nice round numbers covering major subjects like "investigation" and "litigation." The Internal Revenue Service may take a closer interest in these broad-stroke categories.

Early IRS Form 990s reveal a 1983 expenditure of $68,000 for "improvements" on the otherwise unexplained "12th and Newton" property. In the latter half of 1982, Daniel Sheehan acquired a large frame house at 1206 Newton Street, NE—which he deeded over to Sara Nelson the following month.

In October-November of 1982, the Christic Institute induced the District of Columbia to reverse its condemnation of a large run-down home on the corner of 13th and Newton. Despite the "12th and Newton" designation for the expenditure of $68,000 in repairs, it is more likely that the money was spent on the 13th and Newton Street property, 1267 Newton Street, NE, dubbed "Arrupe House."

A call to Arrupe House reveals it to be a sort of group home for men who do not seem to have families, or much of a job. Until his departure for the West Coast to head a newly-formed branch of the Institute, Christic West, this was Father Davis' address. It is also the residence of Andrew Lang, editor of the Christic publication *Convergence,* which reflects that supposedly ideal "convergence" of Christianity and Marxism. Others live there, too. Lang, describing himself as a lay Anglican, says Arrupe House is "an ecumenical community."

During the first half of the Eighties, Father Davis was often to be found gracing the demonstrations which are among the rites of spring, for the leftist community. He can be found yearning to the *Washington Post* for the good old days of the 1960s. By 1985, Davis was signing letters for the activist crazies of Pledge of Resistance.

Yet the snippets of Davis' activities which appear in the public record are far from serious enough to move the Vatican to the reported action of suspending him from priestly duties. Since he is apparently not a womanizer, it seems far more likely that the fault was, and remains, political or ideological, rather than some common moral lapse.

The last big Christic "cause" before they struck gold with La Penca, was Sanctuary.

Christic Comix tells us that Casa Romero, named for Cesar Jerez' candidate for Archbishop of San Salvador, located in Brownsville, Texas, was "the first sanctuary stop of a new 'underground railroad,' a way for churchworkers and friends to shelter and move those who flee for their lives.

"The U.S. does not grant immigration status to political refugees from such 'friendly' countries as Guatemala and El Salvador."

Yes, well, Andy Lang granted that there may have been families of the Salvadoran FMLN guerrillas being smuggled into the United States, to be cared for by goodhearted church people while their menfolk go about doing what Communists do to those who fail to obey. But after all, Lang pointed out, the guerrillas' families are in danger back home, aren't they?

Then let them flee to Nicaragua.

But the Communists have a better idea, and the exploitation of kindly people is a well-known art and craft. Given media and legal protection, a great many of them can be talked into ignoring and overriding the law. The Sanctuary movement gives preference to refugees who speak out against American support for anti-Communists in Central America, and these selected individuals then proceed to tell their benefactors all that the left believes they need to know about the situation.

One has a long wait, if expecting the Christics to adopt the families of the contras, to preserve them from the ire of the Sandinistas.

Let us note, too, that one objective is to deny us control of our own borders, the right to determine by law who enters the country, and to keep the most desultory track of where they go, and what they do. This, it seems, is to be decided unilaterally by people who can mobilize lawyers and a good press for themselves.

Sheehan smelled a new crusade, when Casa Romero needed a lawyer to spring Stacey Merkt, who was using "Bishop Fitzpatrick's own car," with his approval, for "the unlawful transportation of undocumented aliens."

More from Christic Comix. A "Methodist minister" told Sheehan and Father Wally Kasubowski of the Christic Institute that the FBI had warned him that "the sanctuary movement and the Catholic Church are smuggling known terrorists into the U.S." The Methodist continued, "I was told that if the President directed military action in El Salvador, or if we invaded Nicaragua, these Communist terrorists would organize into military cadres . . ."

And then, "A second minister visited, [saying] 'these terrorists would then launch military strikes against army bases, communications centers, and water resource systems in the U.S.' "

Sheehan concluded, "this proves that the U.S. government has a *military* attitude toward the refugees from Guatemala and El Salvador—not a political or an economic attitude, and certainly not a *humanitarian* attitude."

Finally, Father Davis is shown stating darkly, "We have to look into this. He was visited by a different FBI agent. That means someone, somewhere, is making plans."

The Christics purported to be horrified that the government even entertained the notion, for one fleeting moment, that there might be some danger involved in a flood of Central Americans, selected by the American left, entering the country, going who knows where, and doing who knows what. Danny Sheehan was aghast.

Other people might find comfort in entertaining the delusion that anyone is actually minding the store.

"Christic researchers (Kasubowski is shown) discovered that the Federal Emergency Management Agency had extensive and shocking plans which included 'readiness exercises' conducted around the country to prepare to round up, 'in the event of a national emergency' 400,000 undocumented refugees—and put them in ten huge detention camps around the country."

And then they were going to arm "vigilante and right-wing survivalist groups," and then . . . and after that . . .

Although it is getting ahead of our story, it probably ought to be stated, here and now, that all of the above was foamed up in true Sheehan style, to become a Ronald Reagan plot from his days as Governor of California, and to become a subplot, or perhaps a sub-subplot, in the great tapestry of the future La Penca case, complete with eyewitness-type visual detail.

The two ministers and the two FBI agents are among the famous "79 witnesses" kept secret from defense lawyers for eight months. They are also among the twenty who, Judge King stated in his rebuke to the Christics under Rule 11, could not be identified at all!

As for the plan, the author has in hand a copy of the deposition of Louis O. Giuffrida, Director of the Federal Emergency Management Agency, 1981 to 1985—the man traduced by name in Sheehan's story—in which Giuffrida flatly denies the charges.

In short, no evidence.

It hardly seems to matter. We are dealing with a master yarn-spinner here. The *spiel* is delivered with glittery-eyed, fanatic intensity, glib assurance, and at blinding speed. The effect is a hypnotic suspension of disbelief. You can't keep up with it, and he makes it sound so *real*. Sheehan has delivered thrills to those whose spines crawl at the thought of right-wing vigilantes seeking a word with them, and they in turn have delivered large sums of money to the Christic Institute.

People trying to be kind to Sheehan sometimes write that he is a better investigator than lawyer. Gerry Spence suggests that he is a better politician than lawyer. Perhaps someone needs to write that he is a better novelist than lawyer. His *metier* is the medieval morality-play in modern horrorshow form.

Journalist Brian Barger can take credit for a truly historic linkage of forces—when Martha Honey was looking for a free U.S. lawyer of congenial views, Barger suggested Danny Sheehan. According to Barger, he had met Sheehan in 1975, and had done a bit of both journalistic and private business with him in 1985. Thus, Sheehan was fresh in his mind.

It was a perfect match. Sheehan was seeking to enlarge his right-wing fright story, and Avirgan and Honey were more than delighted to assist.

David MacMichael

Although David MacMichael joined the Christic team shortly after the filing of the initial "Sheehan affidavit," we must include him among the creators of the La Penca suit, because he worked with the Christics for a year on its refinement.

MacMichael is not quite like the others. According to the Christics, he fought in Korea as a Marine platoon commander, which makes him a standout, right there. It also makes him about 60 years old. He even led a fairly straight life until recently.

A graduate of the University of Oregon, he currently trades upon his status as a former CIA "contract employee" who is now proud to be on first-name terms with the likes of Sandinista "Gestapo chief" Tomas Borge.

MacMichael was a CIA analyst for two years, 1981–83, and his contract was not renewed. He went public in a clash over his views on the sources of supply of the FMLN guerrillas in El Salvador. He believed that the Reagan administration was exaggerating the degree of Soviet and Sandinista help, for political reasons.

The situation, you see, was more complex than that. Some of the guerrillas carried (and carry) American arms. Now, the standard propaganda line as to how this comes about is one designed to sap morale and turn off public opinion. It is to say that the doughty guerrillas capture their arms, or even buy them, from the no-good lackey soldiers of the imperialists. The line is not served by noting that many of the FMLN guerrillas fought as units with the Sandinistas—and, as such, were happily armed by the Carter Administration, which was so anxious to bring down Somoza.

Nor does David MacMichael, Paladin of Truth, choose to alienate his present patrons by drawing attention to the guns-for-drugs trade on the Communist side. (Fidel Castro was less fortunate. He acknowledged his government's involvement in drug trafficking in 1989.) The Christic line is one of righteous outrage that any crooks on our side ever did such a thing. More than that, of course, their line is that the only crooks in the world are on our side.

Sorry, but the drug trade knows *de nada* about this. One interesting litmus test, these days, is Manuel Noriega of Panama. During the early part of 1989, Christic donors were seen wearing buttons suggesting a Bush-Noriega team occupied the White House.

And then—was it about May or June of 1989?—a sudden silence descended, as Noriega's pals became the Sandinistas and Fidel Castro.

As for MacMichael, his loud defection made him welcome in fifth column circles. Before long, he found the Red side to be the side of the angels, and he joined the Philip Agee Turncoat Brigade.

This is simply a very apt nickname for the group spawned by Philip Agee, the splashiest of the turncoats, role-model for those to come, who showed that you can spill all to the DGI, the Cuban subsidiary of the KGB, and go scot-free. Not only that, but you can earn a comfortable living by publishing books and making the rounds of the college lecture circuit.

Colleges and universities in the United States would rather have Agee come and talk to Tomorrow's Leaders than invite people who fought on our side in the military or intelligence field. This fact was borne upon the late David Atlee Phillips, a high CIA official who, after his retirement, offered his services as a speaker to more than six hundred American institutions of higher learning, and found no takers.

MacMichael, despite his choice of associates, may have a saner, if no less hostile, view of "the major defendants" than Sheehan or Davis. He has been perturbed by the irrationality of Sheehan, his preoccupation with his sup-

48

posedly intuitive understanding of dark forces. MacMichael the non-lawyer seemed more concerned with the viability of Sheehan's "evidence" and the tightness of his case than "the great Harvard constitutional lawyer" himself.

The parting of company came because MacMichael could make no headway. He *wants* the defendants to be destroyed, but he could do little to help a man Who Knows It All.

The Turncoat Brigade

Still, MacMichael is of interest in this account of the Christics because of the strand of radical, activist leftism which he himself represents. Men of the Philip Agee Turncoat Brigade are generally identified in the press as "former intelligence officers," "former CIA officials," or something along those lines. It suggests that they are "in the know"—regardless of how long they have been out of it; at the same time, it *fails* to give us a hint as to whose side they are on now. MacMichael signs ads in Salvadoran newspapers on behalf of the Communist position—signs them with his former CIA affiliation prominently displayed. His "work" in 1989 consists of helping to ensure that the Sandinistas win their promised elections in February of 1990.

Philip Agee, the CIA's first known "ideological defector," says that he began to see things the revolutionary way in 1966. His last assignment was to keep an ear out for defectors, at the Mexican 1968 Olympics. Since he was the one considering defection, this probably did not work out very well.

He then quit the Agency and became an over-age hippie at the flaming red National University in Mexico City. Without protest, he allowed a "swallow," a toothsome Mexican girl with a lot of Cuban friends, to sink her hooks into him, and in 1970–71, he did what he had wanted to do for so long—went to Cuba, and spilled all he could. His objective, he writes, included conveying "information on the CIA to interested Latin American revolutionary organizations . . . efficiently and securely."

Since then, Agee's mission has been to "expose" as many U.S. intelligence officers, agents, assets, and operations as possible. This, you understand, is a crusade against dirty, nasty things like spying and covert action— but in all these years, Agee has never once ferreted out and exposed a single Red agent or operation. It rather makes you doubt his virtuous intent.

In his second book, aptly entitled *Dirty Work,* Agee's major complaint about Agency operations in Western Europe seems to be that the CIA covertly supported the wrong brand of socialism—that of our own Liberal Establishment, rather than Moscow's brand.

Books remain to be written about the effect of that policy on the postwar history of Western Europe. Clearly, it resulted in weakening, crippling, or eliminating more conservative political groups, thereby skewing the entire political spectrum to the left.

Agee was loud in his protestations of innocence when Greek terrorists murdered the CIA Chief of Station in Athens, Richard Welch, two days before Christmas of 1975. Yet, in *Dirty Work,* Agee published a lovingly-detailed account of the murder, as written by the terrorists themselves. He will insist that he merely exposes American agents—it's up to others to do as they will about them. That he is not precisely heartbroken when anti-communists are slaughtered is revealed on page 119 of Agee's third book, *On the Run.* There, he gloats over the death of Congressman Larry P. McDonald (D-Ga.) when the Soviets shot down the Korean airliner in 1983.

Agee disliked Congressman McDonald because he had drawn Congressional attention to his activities. "Through the acknowledgments in my book . . . [he] linked me with people in NACLA, CNSS, IPS, and TNI in a redbaiting harangue that made us look like an international communist conspiracy, in league with terrorists and bent on destruction of the United States."

Without breaking stride to explain about the North American Committee on Latin America, the Center for National Security Studies, Institute for Policy Studies, and Trans-National Institute, trust us, they *are* essentially that, and the linkage was revealed by Agee himself.

Agee's worst was done years ago, and we are to believe that "the wound has been cauterized." But imitators arose early, out of the "anti-war movement" whose members were so notably enthusiastic in their desire for Communist victory in Southeast Asia. Among them we find Louis Wolf.

Counter Spy and *Covert Action*

Wolf claimed "conscientious objector" status in order to avoid fighting—on our side, that is—which is not to say that he missed making the scene! At a 1989 leftist meeting, Wolf told the author that he had been ejected from Laos for "asking far too many questions" about the CIA center from which resistance to the North Vietnamese and Pathet Lao takeover was being directed. The base was, at the time, under the command of Theodore Shackley, one of those selected for sandbagging by the Christic Institute.

Wolf departed Laos for the Philippines, where, he says, he parked himself conveniently close to Clark Air Force Base, in order to run an "anti-war paper'' and do whatever else his views impelled him to do. After a few years, he wore out his welcome in that country, and moved on to London to ''do research.''

Wolf was one of the early people producing *CounterSpy,* a publication which complemented Agee's work in the mid-1970s, and which was initially bankrolled by Norman Mailer. When Mailer could no longer benefit from tax-exempt status for publishing the names of one hundred CIA Chiefs of Station, he lost interest, but Vanessa Redgrave and her British Trotskyites of the Workers' Revolutionary Party soldiered on.

It was then that Wolf teamed with Agee to co-author *Dirty Work.* They appeared in Havana to participate in the ''International Tribunal of the 11th World Festival of Youth and Students'' featuring a ''trial'' of the CIA. Indeed, Agee's book *On the Run* contains photos of him haranguing this Communist audience in Cuba in 1978, as well as delivering a pep-talk to Sandinista troops in 1983. Surely this is wrong. Isn't it also illegal?

On this same visit, Wolf and Agee announced—from Havana, fittingly— the creation of their *Covert Action Information Bulletin,* which is still in existence. If you want confirmation that everything ''we'' do is wrong, dirty, and absurd, this is the rag for you. (Too often these days, summary justice is the only justice in town, and on at least one occasion, it reached Louis Wolf. A few years ago, he was trying to make off with the trash of an anti-communist journalist, Walter Riley. Riley caught up with the nasty little snoop in a stairwell, and Wolf took a tumble down an entire flight of unforgiving metal steps!)

The turncoats have their own organization now, headed by Agee, calling itself the Association for Responsible Dissent (ARDIS). Its vice-president is, or was, Brian Willson, a less intelligent member who distinguished himself by attempting to stop a train with his legs. He was not wearing his ARDIS ''hat'' at the time, but was rather representing Pledge of Resistance.

They are all tied together in a very extensive network. The Christics' MacMichael is a member of ARDIS, and Father Davis publicly supports Pledge of Resistance.

CHAPTER FOUR

SELECTION OF TARGETS

The Christics could have named as defendants hundreds of people who had the misfortune to be included in the work of fiction known as "the Sheehan affidavit," sworn to and filed in U.S. District Court and eventually sold as the June, 1988 publication, *Inside the Shadow Government*. The "racketeering law" allows the most unlikely degree of association to be the basis of a "conspiracy" charge.

Certainly, Sheehan chafed under the restrictions of civil law, which required him to link *any* member of his cast of thousands to the actual bomb at La Penca which injured his client.

Thus, one defendant had to be the bomber himself. Then he would have to be linked to the people Danny Sheehan was *really* after. Sheehan can run on 'til bedtime about "defendant Amac Galil," but, as we have seen, the name itself rests upon what Avirgan and Honey say Carlos told them David said he heard someone say was "Hansen's" real name! By a process known only to Christic mystics, Galil is then fleshed out as a hated right-wing Libyan assassin in the pay of the hated government of Augusto Pinochet in Chile, who was hired by the hated CIA . . .

You can call that evidence—but you'll flunk the bar if you do. On the other hand, if you are aiming for a movie script, you may be doing fine.

As for the selection of other defendants, Avirgan and Honey needed to have faith in their chosen attorney. Both plaintiffs confessed under oath, for instance, that they had never heard of Theodore Shackley and had no knowledge of any wrong-doing on his part. Nevertheless, he was in the suit which was filed on their behalf. Is this justice?

It might appear impossible to connect anybody—other than the fellow journalists at La Penca—with Hansen/Galil, but Sheehan figured to do the job with smoke and mirrors. His clever plan was to tell the court that all his witnesses dwelt in mortal peril and must therefore remain anonymous and out of reach of defense attorneys, while he rummaged through the papers and records of his selected defendants.

He got away with this for quite a while.

More than two years after the suit was first filed, Judge James Lawrence King reached the inescapable conclusion that Sheehan had demonstrated no connection between the bomber, whoever he was, and *any* of the defendants.

On that basis, summary judgment was awarded to the defense. But we are getting ahead of our story.

It is an intriguing question—how did Sheehan choose his very mixed bag of defendants?

One must think of this lawsuit as a shake-bag. You put into it all kinds of people, and expect that the scuzz from the scuzzy ones will dust off onto the others.

Thus we find Colombian "drug kingpins" of world repute, Jorge Ochoa and Pablo Escobar, listed as defendants. It is silly to ask whether they were ever served with a subpoena. The Christics admit that no attempt was made. Father "Gumshoe" Davis' faith did not carry him that far. Escobar and Ochoa were listed as defendants for the scuzz factor. How would *you* like to be listed as co-defendant with that pair, and have it appear in your hometown paper? And have it indexed in the *New York Times,* forever? You see how it works. And then there is the cost of the lawyer you are going to need . . .

An assortment of gun dealers, drug peddlers, and petty offenders were included, to extend the scuzz factor. At this point, the crooks in the group can thank Sheehan for allowing them to boast that they have been cleared in federal court.

His real targets were the men who were causing inconvenience to the Sandinistas and others—Singlaub, Secord, Hull, Calero. Sheehan also had Andy Messing in there, and Rob Owen. Conspicuously absent was Oliver North, although the Communists and their claque were on his case months before the mainline liberals fell into step. If Sheehan did not include North, then why pull Rob Owen through a keyhole, since Owen was merely the courier for North?

The answer is that the Christics deliberately, in true yellow-belly fashion, sought to involve only people who either had no government positions at all, or had retired from government service. That would mean that the Christics would not face government attorneys—and that the defendants, all of them, would be required to go broke paying for their own defense, while the Christics had no trouble passing the plate for tax-exempt grants and donations.

Oliver North was still in service. Rob Owen had no government position. That is why Rob Owen was "lucky Pierre."

Why did Sheehan drop Andy Messing from the case? Messing is more the hate-figure, the subject of a professional trash job by *Regardie's* magazine, than, say, defendant Tom Posey, a good ol' boy ex-Marine who thought the President wanted his help, and was unsuccessfully prosecuted for giving it.

Andy Messing was on the original, May 1986, list of defendants. Like any other defendant, he was first baffled and then horrified to learn—through the telephone calls of reporters—that he was being sued for $23.8 million by perfect strangers. When he tried to talk sense to Sheehan, he was offered a deal—"wear a wire, and ask General Singlaub the following questions"!

No deal!

While he was flattered to be "in the company of men like Singlaub and Shackley," this could in no way cancel out being placed in the shake-bag with big and little drug dealers, since "I've been fighting them in the drug wars since 1979."

Messing had to spend $18,000 on lawyers in a three-month period, before finding two lawyers ready to give him a hand *pro bono*. One was a former prosecutor, Richard Nevitte, who seemed to know how to "reach" Daniel Sheehan—with sweet reason, he says. Since Sheehan had been sent back to the law books by Judge King to put his legal work into acceptable shape, by the time he submitted the case the second time, in the fall of 1986, he had decided to drop Messing.

Messing says his contribution to the contra cause had consisted of the delivery of some 130 tons of medical supplies to Central America. For that, he has had the Internal Revenue Service all over him—whereas the Christics' brood-mates at Quest for Peace are not harassed over the $115 million in supplies they say they have sent to the Sandinistas in Nicaragua.

We shall now look at selected defendants in some detail, so that their lives and careers may be compared to those of the plaintiffs and their Christic team.

Theirs is a different world entirely.

John K. Singlaub

General John Singlaub was born in Independence, California, in 1921, and graduated from the University of California at Los Angeles in 1943. He distinguished himself as Cadet Colonel of his ROTC class, and was commissioned as a lieutenant of infantry on January 14, 1943.

Singlaub immediately volunteered for parachute training, and also became a demolitions officer. In October, 1943, he volunteered again, this time for duty with the Office of Strategic Services, precursor of the CIA. After several months of commando training in northern Scotland in the winter of 1943–44—surely no joy!—Singlaub and two others were selected to be parachuted into the Massif Central of France, to guide resistance actions in support of Operation Anvil-Dragoon, the landings on the Mediterranean coast of France in the summer of 1944.

The OSS case officer for this operation was William Casey, later to become Director of Central Intelligence. Singlaub recalls the lurid but all-too-realistic prospects described, should the Gestapo lay hands upon him, and the offer of a suicide pill. Brashly, perhaps, the 23-year-old warrior rejected it, as it was not his intention to be captured—or, in fact, to be dead, either.

Singlaub's team linked up with the maquisards and saw combat in the south of France.

Later in 1944, Singlaub volunteered to take a small team into Japanese-occupied China and Indo-China, again to train and lead guerrillas. This was an operation where you have to write the book as you go along, staying alive not only in the midst of fanatical enemy forces, but also amid intrigues aimed at altering the postwar picture.

Immediately before the surrender of Japan, Singlaub had the dangerous but gratifying task of parachuting into the Chinese island of Hainan, to rescue some 400 Allied prisoners of war. Nine men, with small arms only, came to dissuade embittered Japanese forces from massacring the POWs—as had already occurred in other areas. Confronting truckloads of Japanese troops, Singlaub faced them down, convincing their officers that the war was indeed over and further rash moves were inadvisable. The POWs were then liberated, while men who had escaped, or evaded capture, and were hiding in the interior of the island were persuaded to come out—to go home again.

Between 1946 and 1948, Singlaub was assigned to Mukden, Manchuria, as Chief of our Military Liaison Mission. This was during the period when Communist and Nationalist forces were struggling for control of all China.

Once more, it was a battle of espionage and intrigue, as well as open warfare. Singlaub's job involved the organization of "stay-behind" spy networks, and this kept him in Mukden until just a little past the "last moment." A message to the top command, recommending that he not be captured, brought in a daring Marine C-46 flight which did not even stop on the runway. Singlaub, his interpreter, and his dog boarded on the run, even as the first Soviet transport aircraft landed.

If one listens to Daniel Sheehan's *spiel,* Singlaub was, at this time, already advancing the criminal conspiracy of the "secret team" by establishing opium-growing in the Golden Triangle. You see, the "secret team" just *knew* that fifteen years down the line, campus leftists would start paying big bucks for a drug habit, the record industry would push drugs on even younger kids, and that in twenty years time, we could demoralize our own armies in the field with the stuff . . . Brilliant!

Well, it makes sense to Sheehan, and to the people who listen to him in slack-jawed awe.

Back to reality. Singlaub spent a few months on the China desk of the youthful CIA, another assignment Sheehan finds sinister indeed. Then came a year at Fort Benning, 1949–50, where Singlaub became executive officer of a battalion of the 82nd Airborne Division. This duty was cut short by the outbreak of the Korean War. He was sent to set up the Ranger training program.

And then it was time to go to Korea. That meant a year as Deputy Chief of the CIA mission, and later he saw combat in the infamous "Iron Triangle." It was here that he won the Silver Star for heroism. Major Singlaub had to take command of an infantry battalion, and "discharged" himself from a field hospital to lead a vital, successful counter-attack. He then reappeared at the hospital with a fresh wound.

The years 1953–57 were spent at Fort Leavenworth. There, after completing the Command and General Staff course, he remained for three years as a member of the faculty. After that came two years as G3 of the 101st Airborne Division, then on to the Air War College.

Promoted to full colonel, he commanded a regiment of the 8th Infantry Division in Germany, and then moved to Seventh Army HQ. This was followed by the obligatory Pentagon time on the Army General Staff.

The night of July 9, 1965, was to be particularly memorable. As a staff colonel, Jack Singlaub was ordered to plan the immediate deployment of American troops to Vietnam! Secretary of Defense Robert McNamara had decided to do *something,* but not enough, to oppose Soviet-sponsored aggression against South Vietnam. Singlaub knew that failure to activate reserves to replace the troops being sent overseas would "signal" to the enemy that we were not serious.

The problem, of course, lay in President Lyndon Johnson's determination to conduct the enormously costly "Great Society" program, with all its opportunities for making political hay on the domestic scene. He was basically uninterested in Southeast Asia, yet within three years, it would defeat him.

Already experienced in war behind the lines in Southeast Asia, Singlaub was sent back there, in charge of a deceptively titled Studies and Observation Group (SOG). He believed in carrying the war into enemy "sanctuaries"— why should they have any? That meant secret operations against the Ho Chi Minh Trail in Laos, and jungle base-camps in Cambodia.

During these years, according to Sheehan, Singlaub was by definition engaging in *crimes* against the Communists, and picking up the threads of his sadly neglected career as a drug kingpin. This is the period when, according to leftist lore, Singlaub was murdering a nice round 100,000 innocents, and smuggling heroin back to the United States in the body-bags of dead American soldiers!

It's tough to run a criminal empire when the Army keeps sending you here and there. Assigned once more to Germany, Singlaub received his first general's star. After that, he went to Fort Hood, Texas, where he took time out from a rather bureaucratic task to learn to fly a helicopter.

Aha! Here it comes, now. On September 21, 1971—a key date in the history of the "secret team"—Singlaub was named Assistant Secretary of Defense for Drug and Alcohol Abuse. See that! The fox was in the chicken-coop.

It was the same thing, you understand, when George Bush, as Vice President of the United States, was supposed to be fighting drugs. The "secret team" was powerful enough to control these positions in order to push their drugs upon a reluctant nation.

From the (actually) thankless task of fighting drugs, Singlaub, now a major general, became commander of US Army Readiness Region VIII. Then, once again to Korea, this time as Chief of Staff of United Nations and all American forces in South Korea.

In that position, Singlaub learned that North Korea's Communist dictator for life, Kim Il-Sung, emboldened by America's withdrawal from Vietnam, was making quite serious preparations for a renewal of the Korean War. The North Korean Army was not only greatly enlarged, but had developed Soviet-style *Spetsnaz* commandos, plus the airlift needed to drop them into South Korea, and even had a submarine force capable of blockading major South Korean ports. An offensive was awaiting the signal.

In August, 1976, a tree in the DMZ, the Demilitarized Zone between North and South Korea, was blocking observation and had to be removed. Unarmed except for the necessary axes, two American officers entered the DMZ and set to work. They were swarmed over by North Korean troops and killed with their own axes.

What ensued might seem like "overreaction," unless one is aware of those very serious preparations made by North Korea, and what they signaled—an intention to move offensively at some point not very far down the line.

South Korean and American forces prepared for war. All ground forces were raised to the highest level of combat readiness, U.S. Air Force units were sent to their advance bases, and the Seventh Fleet was dispatched at flank speed to positions off Korea. The B-52s on Guam went on alert, and fighter-bombers were flown non-stop, with mid-air refueling, from Idaho to Korea.

That was *our* "signal"—expensive, but unmistakable. Kim Il-Sung reconsidered. There was no war. That makes the "signal" not so expensive after all, but rather, a very fine exercise.

At the same time, that *tree* had to go. It could have ranked with Jenkins' Ear as a ridiculous *casus belli,* but the answer, against the background of world-class saber-rattling, was to send a company of South Korean martial-arts specialists with a couple of axes into the DMZ.

No further problem! In fact, the "problem" troubling Jack Singlaub was how to keep other people's meddling from complicating a simple task. He was mindful of the *Mayaguez* incident off Cambodia just the previous year. Then, the Marines sent to retake a hijacked freighter were dismayed to hear, on their tactical net, the unmistakable *basso profundo* voice of Henry Kissinger giving them orders from his Washington office. Singlaub gave his own orders. Under no circumstances were any voices from Washington to bypass him.

What the Communists failed to take, in 1976, was very nearly handed to them in 1977, when the surrender-now artists moved into office with newly-elected President Jimmy Carter. Carter sent a fact-finding team to South Korea to find a careful selection of facts which would justify the withdrawal of American troops. That would be yet another "signal" to the North—

"Y'all come on down!"

"Off the record," General Singlaub said as much to *Washington Post* reporter John Saar, who broke the journalistic rule to write a sensational story. A testy President Carter ordered Singlaub out of Korea *instantly,* without even permitting him to pack. He was summoned directly to the White House "carpet"—and then left sitting in an anteroom while the President decided whether or not to wear jeans for the interview.

Singlaub describes the scene with gentle scorn. As a fashion note, Carter settled for a sports coat and slacks. He then described, in exaggerated fashion, his service as a lieutenant, junior grade, in the peacetime Navy as the seasoning which prepared him for the hard decisions as chief of state.

The General was reassigned to U.S. Army Forces Command at Fort McPherson as Chief of Staff—and, in this role, was sent to Panama to assess the true cost of the transfer of the Panama Canal to the government of Panamanian General Omar Torrijos. That transfer was yet another Carter policy objective.

While investigating this situation, Singlaub became aware of the activities of Torrijos' chief of intelligence, General Manuel Noriega. Noriega had teams of thugs who conducted piracy on the high seas; they boarded American yachts, murdered everyone, loaded the craft with drugs, and sailed straight into American ports. After discharging the cargo, the vessels themselves were simply abandoned.

Such activity was deliberately ignored by the Carter Administration, lest it help to derail the Panama Canal Treaty.

Singlaub was hardly surprised when Torrijos was killed in a mysterious plane crash, with Noriega assuming power in his place. All this knowledge was his a full decade before Noriega's notoriety became public. It makes more absurd than ever the Christic accusation that Singlaub was in league with Noriega. They live in different worlds.

Since Singlaub was not about to bend to the Carterite political breezes, Carter forced him into retirement in June of 1978. Such was the vindictiveness of the President—and his advisors—that confidential orders were given that Singlaub should not be allowed any medical disability pay, despite his accumulation of wounds and injuries in nearly four decades of active service.

Nonetheless, Singlaub retired with more decorations—hard-earned—than can be worn on a body-builder's chest. The Silver Star, of course, the Croix de Guerre with Palm and Star, and so on down to the badges that spell *hombre*—the Combat Infantryman's Badge, the Master Parachutist Badge, and Army Aviator Wings.

In retirement, Singlaub worked privately on national security problems and did some lecturing. Then, in 1981, he founded the U.S. Council for World Freedom, which became the American chapter of the World Anti-Communist League (WACL).

It will be understood that the Christic Institute view of WACL parrots that of Moscow. During 1984–85, Singlaub was chairman of the organization, which, of course, makes him a closet Nazi as well as a career criminal, in the view of the Christics. Evidently, they find it unimaginable that any normal human being could be actively anti-communist.

While active in the leadership of WACL, Singlaub, as a life-long proponent of effective low-intensity fighting, aided the contra resistance to the Communist Sandinista dictatorship in Nicaragua. He did so quite openly, and with the approval of the U.S. government.

It is unfortunate that the CIA, stripped of experienced officers by Stansfield Turner in 1977, first attempted to run a covert war with less than the required number of trained personnel, and was then forbidden to do so at all. This precipitated the full-hearted but doomed activities of Oliver North, who was attempting to "keep the contras alive," as President Ronald Reagan had requested, by whatever means came to hand.

Singlaub, and many other professionals, have been critical of those involved in the "Iran-Contra affair." It was an *ad hoc,* glued-together operation, improperly staffed and, shall we say, unconventionally funded. But a President laid a task upon a man, while a Congress denied him the existing means to do the job.

It is one thing to believe that the contras could have won—and quite another to believe that the American fifth column would have allowed that to happen.

All that the contra effort seems to have produced, for Jack Singlaub, is involvement in the absurd but damaging Christic Institute lawsuit.

Singlaub, who was actually a supporter of Pastora when others thought less of him, still "stands accused" by the loony left of direct involvement in creating the bomb at La Penca!

Theodore Shackley

"Ted Shackley: Key supplier of automatic weapons, ammunition, and C-4 explosives for the contras," say the Christics in their media information packet dated July, 1988.

"As all who do business with me know, I will deal in nothing that 'goes boom or bang,' " declares Ted Shackley in a letter appearing in the *Washington Post* on February 2, 1987.

Nobody other than the Christics have claimed to have a shred of evidence that Shackley had anything to do with the contra operation, much less that he was a "key supplier." More than that, Sheehan's "witnesses," once identified and deposed under oath, deny all knowledge of statements about Shackley which Sheehan has attributed to them.

Daniel Sheehan is doing the best he can to convince the world that Ted Shackley is the mastermind behind the "secret team" which, he claims, hijacked the nation's foreign policy thirty years ago, and has been running it ever since. If you need a master conspirator—and Sheehan does, desperately—what better candidate than the former Associate Deputy Director for Operations, Central Intelligence Agency, who had responsibility for clandestine and covert action worldwide?

As a ranking "spook," and operating under the old rules, Theodore Shackley has spent a lifetime ducking the limelight. He has avoided cameras so well that the Christics' cartoonists are reduced to one (1) photo which must serve all purposes. In the nine-dollar comic-book sold by the Christics, the same photo has dripping fangs here, or is attached to a sinister creature's body there. Like Sheehan, the artist is using his imagination to extend the slender resources at hand.

How do you deal with the fact that Shackley retired ten years ago, and has been in another line of business entirely? Simple. You say that he hired the 800 CIA officers who were laid off in 1977 by the short-sighted Stansfield Turner. Makes sense, doesn't it? By golly, that could account for *everything*.

There is just one small flaw. Can you guess what it is? Right. Sheehan hasn't the smallest scrap of evidence. He is, however, either possessed by the conviction that this is so perfect, it must be true, or else he is doing a favor for people whose identity he has, shall we say, failed to share with us. Perhaps we should ask his mentor, William Davis, if this is so.

James Traub, writing in *Mother Jones,* February/March 1988, noted that "Danny Sheehan is pursuing Theodore Shackley like Captain Ahab with his great white whale." He adds that "Christic investigator David MacMichael likes to jokingly refer to Shackley as 'Professor Moriarty'," Sherlock Holmes' nemesis. "To Sheehan, Shackley is the malevolent puppetmaster of the Secret Team, a 'certified genius' whom Sheehan does not hesitate to compare to Adolf Eichmann."

Small wonder that the Christic iconography, when kindly disposed, portrays the man as Dracula.

Why, the absence of evidence becomes sinister. MacMichael observes darkly, "Shackley does not leave many fingerprints anywhere." Flattering, perhaps—the notion that Shackley can run an army of 800 former CIA officers, and a global criminal empire, without leaving a trace. The Christics cannot seem to accept the more mundane explanation—that he is not doing this!

One by one, Sheehan's "sources" denied the accusations against Shackley attributed to them. They did so long before *Inside the Shadow Government* was published. Yet Sheehan blithely ignores the collapse of his alleged case.

The glacial slowness of the legal system allows anything which once enters the judicial machinery to remain there for many, many years. "Justice delayed is justice denied" means that there is mighty little justice around.

In consequence, Sheehan can come out of left field with a yarn like this and bash his victims for years on end. They must trudge through life charged with, accused of, alleged to be, suspected of, implicated in, and linked with . . .

It can be the purest moonshine, but if press and television people happen to love the story, they are able to spread it to millions, over and over again.

For the victim, it is rather like having a lunatic yapping at one's heels. A lunatic *lawyer.*

Theodore Shackley was born in Springfield, Massachusetts, in 1927, but grew up in Florida. He was just barely old enough to have served in World War II, in Army counter-intelligence in Germany.

He then entered the University of Maryland and obtained a degree in history and political science, plus an ROTC commission—just in time for the Korean War.

He was a Military Police officer, but, thanks to his previous experience and language skills, he was also recruited into the Central Intelligence Agency. Although he hung up his uniform in 1953, Shackley remained in Europe with the Agency until the early 1960s.

He must have built up quite a reputation, because, in the wake of the Bay of Pigs disaster, he was assigned to take charge of what became the largest CIA station in the world—the one in Miami! The Kennedy brothers initiated a clandestine "war" against Fidel Castro, with enormous and enthusiastic assistance from Cubans who had been driven from their homes by the Communist dictatorship.

62

Shackley oversaw these operations. He created the infrastructure within Cuba which made it possible to direct the U-2 spy-plane flights which pinpointed and confirmed the presence of Soviet intermediate-range missiles aimed at American cities.

For this period of service, Shackley received the Distinguished Intelligence Medal.

Operation Mongoose is routinely laid upon Shackley by the Christics. Yet it was "before his time," initiated in November, 1961, and little more than a "paper exercise" before it was phased out in October, 1962. Mongoose involved, among other things, ideas, schemes, and plots for removing Fidel Castro, including by assassination, and it was largely the work of Edward Lansdale. Since matters have been left deliberately murky, Shackley notes that accusations with respect to Mongoose have been a source of "grief and aggravation" over the years.

However, the bare facts of Mongoose were revealed in interim and final reports (11-20-75 and 4-23-76) of the Senate Committee to Study Governmental Operations with Respect to Intelligence Activities, the first relating to "alleged assassination plots involving foreign leaders," and the second relating to the Kennedy assassination.

There was no basis, therefore, for Christic propaganda to insist upon Shackley's responsibility for Mongoose.

In January of 1989, former Secretary of Defense Robert McNamara went to Moscow to chat about old times with Andrei Gromyko. In the course of these chummy reminiscences, McNamara assured the Soviets that there was never any intention to have moves against Castro *succeed*. McNamara said Operation Mongoose was merely a sop to public opinion. Needless to say, this is not the message one passes to the people actually doing the job.

It gets worse. In January, the papers on Mongoose were laid on the table in Moscow and discussed by McNamara and Gromyko—with a clutch of hard-eyed types taking notes, you'd better believe. But it was not McNamara who dug out the records and carried them to Moscow.

The so-called National Security Archive, a far-left organization financed by a very predictable constellation of foundations, is in the business of "mining" the United States government for secrets. David Chang of the National Security Archive told an associate of the author that *they* had taken the documents to Moscow. Apparently, they even run a courier service for the Soviets.

As the clandestine struggle against Castro was being closed down, Shackley went back to Berlin as chief of the CIA base in that outpost city. He was then sent to Laos, to run the quiet but effective effort to keep the Communist Pathet Lao and North Vietnamese forces from taking the whole country, or making uncontested use of the Ho Chi Minh trails. The latter portion of the job was one of intelligence-gathering. Infiltration was monitored, and Hanoi was made to pay a price in attrition.

For the first task, a "war of position and maneuver," Shackley was able to create and effectively employ a tribal army of nearly forty thousand men. This was, by far, the largest covert paramilitary operation in CIA history. This involved "marrying" the guerrillas' activities to tactical air firepower. It was Richard Secord's job to work with the 7th and 13th Air Forces to deliver that firepower when and where it was needed. Secord thereby became part of Sheehan's phantasmagoric "Secret Team"—and a defendant in the La Penca Suit.

Naturally, such a force could not defeat a modern army, but it could contest its advance and exact a cost. The effort was not appreciated by the Communists.

And lo, we find Daniel Sheehan saying, in papers actually filed in the federal court in Miami, that Shackley's activity in Laos was "to organize, fund, and direct a secret criminal army composed of Hmong (or Meo) tribesmen. This army, with bases throughout northern Laos, was . . . to fight the Communist Pathet Lao insurgent forces within Laos." Conveniently omitted from Sheehan's summary are the North Vietnamese regulars who were also on the scene.

And this appears as an element of a "racketeering" charge. Incredible! But it certainly tells the world where Danny Sheehan is coming from.

A different view of the Laotian operation is offered by Angelo Codevilla, formerly with the Senate Intelligence Committee and now at the Hoover Institution on War, Revolution, and Peace. In a paper on political warfare, Codevilla says:

> The war in Laos by the H'mong was for an indisputably just cause, was waged competently, and had solid effect. In short, it was something to be proud of, something that a US government committed to victory should have been trumpeting to the Western world . . . But it was kept a secret from the American people and from much of the US government because the highest authorities had not mustered the moral self-confidence to argue that the Communist side and all who stood with it deserved to be defeated.

64

Elements of the US government, Codevilla asserts, were not only "unwilling to use the war in Laos as a badge of honor," but even more, he faults them for "avoid[ing] a direct confrontation with the pro-Communist faction in the US establishment." Former U.S. Ambassador to Laos G. McMurtrie Godley, writing in the *Wall Street Journal* (16 September 1987) cited the CIA operation in Laos for "technical proficiency" and as a model of "effective and timely communication between the executive and legislative branches."

Shackley's "reward" for doing well in Laos was to be made CIA Chief of Station, Vietnam, where he served from December 1968 to early 1972. The fact is, no man in the history of the CIA has run more big stations in times of crisis than Shackley.

But, according to Sheehan, Shackley spent this time advancing his career as a master criminal, and murdering "forty thousand people," although sometimes the Christics like "sixty thousand" better.

Sheehan is referring, here, to CIA Director William Colby's Phoenix program, intended to identify and root out the Viet Cong infrastructure—the covert VC who dominated the rural population through sickening terror. In his recent book, *Lost Victory,* Colby explains the program in detail. All pro-Communist propagandists, including Sheehan, describe these covert VC terrorists as "mayors, clerks, teachers, business professionals, and educated persons." They have it wrong. Those were the people the VC were killing.

"Phoenix had many fathers," Bui Diem, former South Vietnamese Ambassador to the United States, told the author, "But Mr. Shackley was not one of them." Actually, Shackley emphasized getting back to intelligence basics, leaving it to the military to fight the war. In short, contrary to the claims of the radical left, neither Shackley nor Singlaub were the driving force behind the Phoenix program. Colby was.

Perhaps it is also worth mentioning that guerrillas—non-uniformed irregulars—cannot really claim to be innocent civilians merely because they try to pass as such. International law has unkind things to say about *francs tireurs.*

Then, returning to Washington, Shackley headed the Western Hemisphere Division of the CIA's Operations Directorate. In this capacity, the Christics insist, he was the villain who liberated Chile from Salvador Allende and his foreign legion of Communist supporters. This, in Communist and Christic eyes, was dastardly. But the Chileans were delighted with it as the author saw first hand in 1974.

Unfortunately for Sheehan's yarn, Shackley had been shifted over to head the East Asia Division some four months before Allende found himself deposed, and opted to commit suicide in La Moneda. Perhaps Sheehan is distressed because Shackley was awarded his second Distinguished Intelligence Medal in 1973.

As head of the East Asian Division, Vietnam was back on Shackley's plate. He had the sad job of viewing from afar "the last days of Pompeii."

Asked why we lost in Vietnam, he says, "There was no will to win." After we had taught the Vietnamese how to fight a modern war, he says, the means to do so were withdrawn from them.

The comment carries one's thoughts back to McNamara's January revelations in Moscow. There was no "will to win" in Cuba, at the level of Secretary of Defense, if we are to believe Mr. McNamara.

By the mid-1970s, Shackley was within range of possible promotion to Director of Central Intelligence. Under George Bush's directorship, he became Associate Deputy Director for clandestine operations, and it was bruited about that, had Gerald Ford won the 1976 presidential election, the plum might have fallen to him.

The sappers went to work, using anything to chip away at Shackley's reputation. President Carter appointed Stansfield Turner as Director, and in 1977, Turner gutted the clandestine service, firing some 800 veteran officers. Still ranking as Associate Deputy Director, Shackley was moved to "the intelligence community," where CIA, DIA, NSA and others gathered. Then, after 28 years, he retired in 1979.

However, there was always a cold fear in certain circles that Shackley might reappear on the scene, even though the "threat" diminished with the passage of time. Sheehan evidences this fear in his constant insistence upon a long-standing "criminal" link between Shackley and Bush. They, according to him, have been in the drug racket together for a decade or more . . .

According to the Christic Institute comic-book version of events, Shackley hired all the dismissed officers, and continues to run a vast private criminal conspiracy. The Christics have thousands of little people out there who are madly in love with this story, and will send money to hear the next thrilling chapter.

On another level, they have dozens of key moneybags, most of whom are not really stupid. They are delighted with the story for its sheer destructiveness.

Since his retirement, Shackley has become a successful oil market analyst.

He really doesn't need all these Christic accusations. Naturally, they hurt business. And the necessity to spend money on lawyers to beat off these people is both distracting and a drain.

Of course, that was the Christics' intention. After all, this is the Great White Whale, Professor Moriarty, and Adolf Eichmann rolled into one, and Sheehan is gonna *get* him!

Shackley, as noted, adheres to the old rules, and does not expect to rush into print with a tell-all book of his own any time soon. There was a nice try from some journalist who wrote to him on *Nation* stationery, of all things, on a day when the author was conducting an interview.

Trust me, said the *Nation* writer, I'll be fair. I want to do "a biography of your life."

Shackley smiled and said, "Tell him thanks, but I already have several contracts on my life."

Richard Secord

Retired Air Force Major General Richard Secord was born in rural Ohio in 1932. He entered West Point in 1951 and graduated with the Class of 1955, becoming an officer in the United States Air Force.

The peacetime Air Force, looking toward the opening of the new United States Air Force Academy at Colorado Springs, was interested in having West Point-trained officers to stiffen the new faculty. Secord was selected for graduate training, and obtained a Master's degree in English literature at the University of Oklahoma.

But he was a flying officer at heart, facing the prospect of being converted into a professor of English! Small wonder that he leaped at the opportunity for secret Air Commando work in Southeast Asia instead. Ultimately, he would become a specialist in flying close ground support, with 300 missions to his credit.

Of course, our enemies—abroad and at home—would not consider this creditable, much less heroic. The Distinguished Flying Cross means nothing to them. One may question, for instance, whether leftist author Leslie Cockburn, so snidely critical of Secord, has ever had to press on with a mission, however hair-raising, or whether she has ever been in actual fear for her life. Has she ever had to remain calm and function correctly while filled with the conviction, "I'm gonna die"?

Unfortunately, our nation sports thousands of professional propagandists who are pleased to denigrate those who have demonstrated their courage in the service of their country.

Let us recall that 1962 was a time when the Kennedy Administration was enthusiastically engaging in a number of secret wars. Those currently deploring "covert operations" are generally careful not to lay them at the feet of such liberal saints as the Kennedy brothers, who were great enthusiasts of same. Guerrilla and counter-guerrilla warfare, "counter-insurgency,"— these were the buzz-words of plugged-in "defense intellectuals" cranking out books by the shelfload, because the defense dollars were there to pay for them.

In such a milieu, flying AT-28s and A-37B ground-attack aircraft is where the action was—flying close to an unpitying terrain, home to ground forces who didn't like you either, and flying these missions at night, or through solid, blinding sheets of monsoon rain.

This is where Richard Secord was to be found during the 1960s, when so very many other young Americans were being taught, in their colleges and universities, to hate America. Great numbers of these young Americans were also hiding from the possibility of having their own lack of courage brought to the attention of themselves and others—and they know it. How very much more satisfying it was to adopt a pose of high moral principle! An overly generous nation indulged them in it. From these ranks are drawn the likes of the Christics.

After learning the ground-support trade in Vietnam in 1962, Dick Secord was destined for another scene of secret warfare—Iran, in the middle 1960s. Secord had three successive six-month tours as one of two Air Force officers in an 80-man Special Forces team helping the Shah to defeat a Kurdish insurgency.

The Kurds have the misfortune to live in an area where Turkey, Iran, and Iraq abut. They would like to have a country of their own, but none of the above three governments are interested in giving up large chunks of national territory, merely to please the Kurds.

The Middle East has seen thousands of years during which central governments have crushed troublesome minorities in a merciless manner, and the custom continues, with or without an American involvement. The Soviet government, which had tried to annex northwestern Iran in 1946, was encouraging a Kurdish leader, Mullah Mustafa Barzani, to raise the standard of an independent Kurdistan in one or another of the three countries involved, simply to weaken any pro-Western neighboring government.

The Turks apparently lived up to their no-nonsense reputation all too well, so that the softer targets appeared to be Iran and Iraq. As these governments nurtured their own hostilities against each other, they, too, encouraged the Kurds to fight their battles in the other fellow's country. This bled the Kurds white, in the postwar era. At various junctures, the United States has covertly dabbled in the game, too, and this is what brought Dick Secord to Iran, 1963 to 1965.

After that, it was back to Southeast Asia for the remainder of the 1960s, for what Danny Sheehan and Leslie Cockburn are pleased to describe as a nefarious career of "racketeering."

Secord points to a paragraph on page 101 of Cockburn's hasty trash-job, *Out of Control,* which is wall-to-wall lies. She purports to be discussing the period 1966–68. It reads:

> The air wing commander for Laos was an air force lieutenant colonel named Richard Secord. Secord's specialty, then and later, was air transport of the variety that requires secret movement of secret cargoes. His superior at the Special Operations Group was Col. Harry C. ("Heinie") Aderholt.

At the time, Secord states, he was a major, and there was no "air wing," his specialty was never "air transport," and his superior was never Colonel Aderholt. Aside from that. . .

Major Secord, among others, was engaged in trying to prevent the Communists from taking over the whole of Laos, rather than just the half which had been awarded to them by Averill Harriman in the 1962 agreement which left them the part of Laos they needed most, at the time—the part with the Ho Chi Minh Trail.

Sheehan and his literary shill, Leslie Cockburn, find that the purposes of "docudrama" are best served by placing Oliver North in Southeast Asia, engaged in "racketeering" along with his elders in the story, at a time when he was still at the U.S. Naval Academy in Annapolis. Since both of these fiction-writers have only a dim notion of what fledgling Marine platoon commanders do (aside from murdering inoffensive civilians, that is), they would have us believe that North was some sort of hoodlum working for the freebooting drug lords of Laos. In actuality, all of the men traduced by Sheehan and Cockburn were demonstrating considerable prowess and courage.

After promotion to lieutenant colonel, Secord took command of a squadron of A-37B Dragonfly ground-support aircraft, 1969–71. These are tiny aircraft, but they carried a heavy external load of ordnance. Ask a flier what you can carry in them and the answer is "a pilot." Period. If you would like Sheehan and Cockburn to look upon you with favor, you could believe that the pilots were conveying opium to market in their laps.

Ms. Cockburn, who might be called unworldly, to put the best face upon it, assumes that the warriors in Laos wore gold for the same reason that ghetto kids drape themselves in gold chains—to show that they are rich drug dealers. She sneers at the gold bracelets and watchbands as though you couldn't fool *her*.

Not quite. The gold was worn in case of a possible crash landing among primitive tribesmen who don't speak your language, but do know gold when they see it, and would patch you up and guide you out for the promise of more.

In 1972, Secord obtained a second Master's degree, this one in international affairs, from George Washington University. He then became a full colonel, serving a three-year tour in the Pentagon, learning to fly a desk, an unfortunate adjunct of rank. But it earned him a general's star; at 43, Secord was the youngest brigadier general in the Air Force.

The year 1975 saw him return to Iran, where he would assist with the arming and equipping of the Iranian Air Force. This is a period during which Sheehan and Cockburn claim, on the basis of yarns spun by a "witness" paid $20,000, that Secord was engaged in more criminal skulduggery.

Whatever he was doing seems to have earned him a second star, and another tour at the Pentagon, this time as Director of International Programs for the Air Force, 1978–81.

During this period, Secord was tapped for a quiet job; after the Desert One hostage-rescue fiasco in Iran early in 1980, there was a need to create a second task force which might do it better. Secord helped to put together, and then commanded, a secret joint Army-Air Force unit for the job, should the folks in the Carter White House ever recover their nerve. That didn't happen. But America's fifth columnists sneer at Secord, not Carter.

The Summer 1987 issue of Louis Wolf's *Covert Action Information Bulletin,* the publication for spy-propagandists for the Communists, devoted five pages to a hate-fest directed at any and all elite U.S. strike units. These people can put a negative spin on absolutely anything. Authors Ellen Ray and William Schaap imply that failure of the first hostage-rescue mission was a high-level plot by Generals John Vessey and John Singlaub to make President Carter look bad.

In 1981, the Great AWACs Flap arose, when Israel strenuously objected to the proposed sale of Airborne Warning and Command aircraft to Saudi Arabia. In hopes of defusing the political uproar, it was decided to place an active-duty military officer in the position of Deputy Assistant Secretary of Defense for a vast region, inluding the Middle East, and let him thrash it out with Congress. Secord did so, successfully, and was awarded the Defense Distinguished Service Medal.

Cockburn is no better on medals than on military aircraft. She remarks that General Secord, "for his efforts received the Distinguished Service Medal, generally awarded for valor in war." Not only is that incorrect—the DSM is the highest armed forces decoration for peacetime service—but the Defense Distinguished Service Medal is different. Secord holds both and received a second Defense Distinguished Service Medal from Secretary of Defense Caspar Weinberger personally.

Secord retired for a variety of reasons, some of which had to do with reservations about policy. Most men who have served from, say, the age of 20 to 50, look forward to a fresh career, rather than a life of ease.

Secord did a bit of consulting, then settled into a business with Albert Hakim, an Iranian-born American later seen on TV during the Iran-Contra hearings. They were offering to friendly Mideast countries "ballistically-hardened aircraft shelters, communications, POL, and air defense systems."

When the call came to run the contra air supply operation, this was not something Secord was particularly eager to do. And, being retired and in business for himself, of course he had to see a profit in it. Everybody knew this was a job the CIA normally would have handled had Admiral Turner not gutted America's capabilities during the Carter years. Instead, it became something glued together out of aircraft and pilots wherever they could be picked up in a hurry. Secord accepts blame for the inadequacies of his subordinates in the field, saying he was simply slow to recognize them. However, the air support was becoming effective, and was still reasonably secret, when the C-123 was shot down, with Eugene Hasenfus the only survivor.

"They had a damned library aboard that plane," Dick Secord says in disbelief, referring to the identification, logbooks, business cards, phone numbers, *ad infinitum* to be picked from the wreckage. He calls it "a shocking violation of established procedure."

Hasenfus saw no reason to make things tough on himself, so he gave the Sandinistas all the information they wanted and they let him go home for Christmas.

Nonetheless, there is another aspect to things.

At Lourdes, Cuba, there is a signal intercept facility which monitors the airwaves in the same manner as our National Security Agency at Fort Meade, Maryland. It monitors our voice and data traffic, and is "very up-to-date and sophisticated." In addition, the land lines and microwave circuits for all of Central America pass through Managua.

Dick Secord believes that some of the material used in Sheehan's "docu-drama" affidavit, the non-fiction part, may have been fed to him indirectly from Lourdes intercepts.

Would the Christics have turned it down if it had been handed to them by a Soviet KGB general in full dress uniform? More likely, Danny Sheehan would have felt flattered beyond words. The desire for discretion would come from the other direction.

John Hull

John Hull was born in Patoka, Indiana, in 1920. The Hulls were—and are—a farming family, although John Hull's father later became involved in agricultural extension work and in some agriculturally-oriented projects of the Ford Foundation.

In 1937, John Hull learned to fly; he and his brother were able to share a Piper Cub. At the University of Evansville, in 1939, he entered the Civilian Pilot Training Program, advancing steadily to the level of instructor. Forgetting about schooling, he and his brother were in California, in 1940, training young Air Corps pilot-candidates, but this was not challenging enough.

The summer of 1941 found him in Canada, where he joined 45 Group North Atlantic—a Royal Air Force unit using civilian ferry pilots. Hull spent the war flying plywood Mosquito light bombers and B-24 heavy bombers across the Atlantic to England. This was not easy! A small unit, the 45th had a very high casualty rate.

The ferry route was a series of hops into ever-filthier weather—Labrador, Greenland, Iceland—and the Mosquito was apt to go out of control with a relatively thin coating of ice. The "point of no return" loomed up early and often. Greenland is either vertical or ice, and had only two airstrips at the time. The most notorious involved a dogleg approach up a canyon-like fjord, and if it were fogged in—too bad. The "alternate" was on the other side of the icecap, much too far away.

So that is what John Hull was doing, during World War II. When he returned to Indiana in mid-1945, his American draft board wanted to draft him! Instead, he used a high-ranking RAF connection and obtained a job teaching people in India how to fly B-24s.

But the Pacific war was soon over, as well. John Hull returned to the farm; he and his brother also ran a flying school, and occasionally flew with the Cole Brothers' Flying Circus.

About 1960, Hull and his retired father loaded their Cessna 180 with soil-testing equipment and went all around Central and South America, checking out soil types.

About ten years later, Hull returned to a portion of Costa Rica which had looked exceptionally good, and bought 1700 acres of land, 1600 of which was still forest. This he and his father cleared and farmed, later taking on the management of other farms in the area as well. Hull's father died and was buried in Costa Rica in the mid-1970s.

For the information of the whiners, demonstrators, "social critics," "advocacy lawyers" and their flag-burning clients, this is called "productive activity."

Costa Rica is a lovely country, with nice if not overly ambitious people. Politically, it is a weak country, one which has prided itself on not having an army, and with a government so easily manipulated by outside forces as to be a week-to-week political weathervane. It does not have to be economically feeble, but it is; evidently, no Costa Rican government has seen a loan it didn't like, so it is currently drowning in unrepayable debt. Uncle Sam is subsidizing the country to the tune of a million dollars a *day*.

If you think this buys loyalty, think again.

If leftists are "in," then the government will accept the services of veterans of the Allende government, such as John Biehl, advisor first to Allende, and now to Costa Rican President Oscar Arias. This despite the total shambles which Allende and his government of domestic and imported Reds made of Chile in their day

The Costa Rican government apparently reveled in the sport as "everybody" took up Somoza-bashing in the late 1970s—and that means the Carter Administration worked hand in hand with the Communists to depose Somoza, and replace his government with the Sandinistas.

Just so, Fidel Castro was supposed to represent an improvement over Batista. People like the Christics still think he is.

Costa Rica played very much the same role of staging area for attacks on Nicaragua during the campaign to "get" Somoza as it did, however briefly, for the contras. But John Hull had refused to aid the Sandinistas, recognizing them as Communists. For anyone with ten or twelve years' worth of memory, the current spectacle of Costa Rica endeavoring to reclaim its political innocence is quite amusing.

Hull was drawn into these affairs largely because of the location of the farms he had owned and managed for up to twenty years, which are close to the Nicaraguan border. He had airstrips, because people who can possibly arrange to do so get around that region by air. It takes the Christics to convert any set of circumstances into a long-term criminal conspiracy.

Because of Congressional fumbling, interference, and worse, the effort to "reach" the Sandinistas by the only means they understand became a lurching, on-again, off-again exercise. What Oliver North and his quickly cobbled-together support organization was trying to do was to impart a minimum of continuity to this effort, in the wan hope that Congress would regain its senses.

When support for the Contras was "on," Congressionally approved, John Hull cooperated, allowing his airstrips to be used for their support, meaning the movement of supplies in and casualties out, although he was still running his farms, and using his own plane for the usual purposes, which included mercy-flights for local people in need of medical care quickly.

When Congress caved in to organized leftist pressure, the kind of pressure that wins wars for the Communists in Washington instead of in the field, Hull continued to cooperate in the effort to keep resistance alive. Not being a leftist lawyer, he probably thought that the President of the United States retained his constitutional right to conduct the foreign affairs of the United States.

In 1984, at the strong suggestion of the Central Intelligence Agency, John Hull acquired a dual citizenship, becoming a Costa Rican citizen, thus placing himself somewhat at the mercy of a fickle Costa Rican government—and an American government apparently going through another phase of leaving its people twisting in the wind, when not actively participating in the lynching-bee.

In 1985, Avirgan and Honey began their accusations and legal harassment, later abetted by Danny Sheehan and Father Bill Davis. Hull has been smeared and hounded ever since. As leftist power increases in Costa Rica—the country which takes pride in its defenselessness, which could therefore be "had for breakfast" by Nicaragua, and which has seen quite enough of the palsied hand of Uncle Sam lately—Hull has found himself treated very badly indeed

74

in Costa Rica.

After the *La Penca* book was published in Costa Rica in 1985, John Hull sued Avirgan and Honey for libel. Thinking he had an open-and-shut case, he walked into his first Christic legal buzz-saw. The defendant, Avirgan, was present in the courtroom—orchestrating lights and cameras. The judge allowed the defendants to present their evidence, and did not allow the plaintiff to present his! Hull saw how it lay, and says he did not feel able to outbribe the Christics, so he lost. He could hardly have known that *La Penca* was just the beginning of the Christic extravaganza.

Robert Owen

"You think it can't be that bad. You think you can make a difference."

These were, somehow, Rob Owen's most memorable words to the author. Such words tend to take you back to when you thought the same about your country.

But, despite changes here and there, we find that Philip Agee, professional turncoat, is durable on the college lecture circuit, while when Rob Owen appears at his own *alma mater,* Stanford University, and speaks in a manner normal for an idealistic American, the reaction is described as, "Is this guy for real?"

This is the campus that says, "Hey, hey, ho, ho, Western Civ has got to go."

They demoralize and they brainwash at Stanford these days. If there are people on the Stanford faculty or administration who resent that accusation, as distinct from smirking in self-satisfaction, let them reclaim their institution first.

Rob Owen gained either fame or notoriety, depending upon whose side you are on, during the Iran-Contra hearings. But, because of his inclusion in the *La Penca* suit, we know that Owen had come to the attention of Avirgan, Honey, and Sheehan before that story broke. He was included in their lawsuit because he was opposing the Sandinistas, and hardly because they seriously thought he was involved in drug-peddling.

Robert Owen was born in Providence, Rhode Island, in 1953. This makes him a very full generation younger than the other defendants.

He served in no wars—Vietnam was essentially over before he came to maturity. The contra cause was his war. He served in a "staff" capacity, but he has felt made-in-Washington defeat as keenly as a veteran of any of our other no-win wars since 1945. He shares in the feelings of pain, betrayal, and impotent rage at the astounding political power of an entrenched and brazen American fifth column.

Owen also differs from the other defendants in being a "preppie." He attended Phillips Academy, in Andover, Massachusetts, did some traveling, studied in Britain, worked at another prep school—St. Paul's, in New Hampshire—and obtained his degree in political science from Stanford University in 1978.

Preppie, yes, wimp, no. He is a big, rugged man who tried repeatedly, and in a most determined manner, to enlist in the Marine Corps, but has never been acceptable to the military because he had wrecked his knee in contact sports; he had additional surgery in 1989.

In 1980, Owen gave up a job as Director of Admissions and college counselor at the Brentwood School in Los Angeles in order to go to Thailand to help with the problem of the refugees from Communist terror in Cambodia. Most people are aware of who did the massive killing, but the left blames "us" anyway.

He entered into national Republican activity in 1981, became Legislative Assistant to then-Senator Dan Quayle in 1982, and moved on to Gray and Company Public Communications, a public-relations firm, in 1983. From there, he became drawn into the contra support effort run from the National Security Council by Lt. Col. Oliver North in 1984, and was taken on as a Department of State consultant on humanitarian aid in 1985. This is not quite the checkered past it seems, as certain jobs flowed into each other.

As "the Courier" for Oliver North, Rob Owen carried money and messages back and forth to Central America and around the United States. We are offered various "atrocity stories"; it is said that he once witnessed the loading of an aircraft with arms destined for the contras, at a time when one of the Boland amendments was in effect.

We are invited by the Christics to consider this a criminal act. We are told that Owen actually carried information on the base location of the murderous Hind helicopters which the Soviets had sent to Central America. Why, quite possibly North, the veteran Marine, had offered some pros and cons as to the price that might have to be paid by brave men, to save other brave men by destroying the Hinds on the ground. In the Christic book, a crime!

Taking out the Hinds was not even attempted, by the way, but just carrying a message about it is enough to put you on a list, and not merely in the Communist capitals, but here at home, too.

So you wake up one morning to find yourself in a civil racketeering suit, with some radical lawyer dragging your dead brother into it, as well. In the old days, a Sheehan would keep folks mesmerized around the peat fire through a long Irish winter, stringing it all together, telling how Owen's brother had died working the criminal rackets with North in Vietnam, in league with those other "major defendants." Nowadays, he puts it into a lawsuit, for the profitable titillation of the Hollywood left.

Rob Owen's brother died in Vietnam, delivering rearguard covering fire which allowed others to live. He had nothing to do with Oliver North—Vietnam is a big place, would you believe. But Sheehan and the mass media understand "docudrama," that blend of fact and fiction which tells an absorbing tale and which, above all, puts across a political propaganda message.

The rest is more public "history." Congressional Democrats tasted blood, and saw an election looming, while the hard left had an agenda no different from before—division and defeat. People like Daniel Sheehan do not merely dream of bringing down an American government in order to save a communist government. They work at it, very hard. But if you ask them what they are about, they tell you they are standing upon moral principle.

Rob Owen made a good impression on the public, during the Iran-Contra hearings. He has received painful, yet ultimately valuable lessons about having to face avowed enemies to the front, while the knife descends from above and behind.

CHAPTER FIVE

LA PENCA: THE LANDMARK CASE
THAT WASN'T

Because the case ended, at least in District Court, with summary judgment for the defense, there is little need to argue the charges here.

We can demonstrate the spurious nature of the more egregious or amusing efforts. But we must also look at the Christic objectives, which were far broader than winning a multi-million-dollar lawsuit. And some of the tactics are instructive.

Immediate Objectives

Martha Honey wanted a U.S. lawyer—free, of course—who would sue John Hull in an American court.

Daniel Sheehan wanted a plaintiff as an excuse to fight the enemies of the Sandinista regime in court, and his wife, Sara Nelson, could see the money rolling in, if they did.

The immediate battle, at the time, was to end contra aid. By 1989, of course, the contras were yet another anti-Communist army abandoned by the U.S. government. The Christics can claim credit for a large contribution to this Communist objective.

Whether Danny Sheehan dreamed from the beginning of bringing down the Reagan Presidency with his lawsuit is unclear, but he did express this hope soon after filing the suit. The notion of bagging a President of the United States would seem worthy of his ego.

As time went on, it was also his publicly-expressed wish, hope, and determination to prevent the election of George Bush, or failing that, to bring him down in some manner. Bagging two Presidents of the United States— who could follow such an act?

Long-Term Objective: Blocking American Covert Action

Halting any covert action on the part of the United States is a standard objective of Soviet *dezinformatsiya;* the hottest criticism of covert action is from people whose faces go blank at mention of the KGB.

There is a permanent campaign against the mere concept of covert action. This refers to action with more muscle than "diplomatic pressure," but less than open military clobbering. It is useful for protecting friendly governments, blocking the development of bad situations, and taking care of minor messes without great fuss and clamor.

To halt *American* covert action against the *Communists* is a goal of the Communists, naturally, and all their true friends, just as naturally.

Because this is so obvious, the cleverer of these Communists and true friends will occasionally note that other forces in the world also conduct covert actions. But the nature of the evenhandedness is a giveaway. There will be a lengthy peroration against American acts, complete with as many names and details as possible, and as much primitive emotionalism as possible (brutal, corrupt, rape, torture). There will be expressions of regret that the national honor has been so stained—and all for naught, as "covert action never works."

After that, it *may* be admitted that vague other forces in the world, unfortunately, do vague things that are not nice. They are provoked to such behavior by our own evil actions (although in recent years it has become okay to blame Stalin, too—in moderation). The listener will be assured that Stalin's covert action never worked, either. Trust us, would we lie to you?

So there you have it, folks. We're passing out these cards, and we are asking you to write to Congress to Stop Covert Action Now. Demand that *Uncle Sam* be the one required to play the game with his cards face up.

The audience—and speakers—then file out past tables groaning under the weight of "literature" supporting Communist-oriented or directly sponsored covert actions.

This educational vignette is from a meeting addressed by Daniel Sheehan at Johns Hopkins University in April, 1989. It was chaired by Sheehan's good friend Sue Wheaton, wife of the Rev. Phil Wheaton, who finds welcome in Castroland, and who writes for Louis Wolf's *Covert Action Information*

Bulletin. Mrs. Wheaton avers that she is not responsible for the publications distributed at her meetings. She could not have objected to the presence of the Turncoat Brigade, since Louis Wolf was another of her speakers, and David MacMichael a third.

The Trotskyites, fresh from their newfound welcome in the Soviet Union? No problem. Pledge of Resistance, supported by Father Davis? No problem. Baltimore Emergency Response Network, with its list, forwarded to the Nicaraguan *comandantes,* of volunteers available for service to the Sandinistas? No problem. Yet Sue Wheaton and the Rev. Chester Wickwire, "chaplain emeritus" of Johns Hopkins University (and known to the faculty as "Wickedwire"), say they do not know where the Weather Underground material came from.

It's quotable stuff. Perhaps they ought to ask Louis Wolf about it. Husband Phil Wheaton *and* the terrorists publish in Wolf's *Bulletin,* and all seem to agree with Wolf's new formulation that "anti-terrorism is the McCarthyism of the 1980s."

"Resistance is not a crime," the terrorists scream, "resistance" taking the form of gunpoint "expropriations," a bombing here and there, that sort of thing. For $2.50, you can order "all communiques issued by the United Freedom Front, the Armed Resistance Movement, the Revolutionary Fighting Group, and the Red Guerrilla Resistance, which accompanied armed actions."

There is a two-page listing of misunderstood terrorists currently languishing in assorted U.S. prisons who would like pen pals, and *somebody* thought that the clientele attending Sue Wheaton's anti-covert action meeting would sympathize with them. Without Sue Wheaton, we might have missed all this.

Have pity on the self-sacrificing terrorists. After all, "many were captured trying to build revolutionary organizations that were armed and clandestine." Some were even victims of the domestic intelligence program which bagged the perpetrators of some of the "literally hundreds of bombings of government, military, and war-corporate targets. It was the full range of these activities that . . . made [the anti-war movement] a real ally of the Vietnamese [Communists]."

If you like, you can write to the information office in Germany which will put you in touch with a pen pal from the Red Army Fraction, or Baader-Meinhof gang . . .

This literature is brought to you by the folks who say that armed resistance to *Communism* constitutes criminal racketeering. Is it crystal clear whose side they are on?

RICO: Weapon of Choice

Every prosecutor or plaintiff's lawyer reaches for it now, if he possibly can.

As Christic consultant David MacMichael chortled, "The way Blakey [Robert Blakey, 'father of RICO'] wrote it, any five people with Italian names exchanging Christmas cards are a racketeering conspiracy."

The original idea, back in 1970, was to produce a new tool against the Mafia. In the 1970s, the law was used hesitantly, for some reason, and without much effect on mobsters.

In the 1980s, the joys of RICO for other purposes were discovered, and the result is that a messy divorce can become a civil racketeering case; loss of a job, a lost contract, almost *anything* can be cast in RICO terms, and if the judge is not quick to dismiss it, it can become immured in the judicial system for years.

Even if without merit, until a judge says as much, the case represents a legal war of attrition.

And Blakey deliberately stacked the legal deck in favor of the prosecution, in criminal RICO cases, or the plaintiff, in civil RICO cases. The defendant, even if innocent, cannot collect damages from his legal assailant, while the plaintiff in a civil case, or prosecutor in a criminal case, can demand triple damages.

Under criminal RICO, the prosecutor can also tie up the defendants' assets *in advance*. Sheehan would have loved to do that—to paralyze his victims for the multi-year duration of the case, win or lose—but he is not quite yet the "people's prosecutor" he would like to be.

In *all* civil cases, the rules of evidence are looser than in criminal cases. Proof "beyond reasonable doubt" becomes merely "the preponderance of evidence." Thus, if a hair over half of what Sheehan says is credible to a jury, he wins.

RICO is made to order for the legal terrorists. And so we find, in Christic Comix, Sara Nelson deciding that the contra effort should be attacked as a racketeering conspiracy—the Contra Nostra, ha-ha. In the next panel, we find Daniel Sheehan preferring his term, "the secret team." He won.

Claims

Avirgan and Honey, plaintiffs, and the Christics had a rollicking good time in shaping their claims. They came up with a fat price-tag on *everything,* even down to the "cost" to Martha of taking care of her children, when Tony should have been doing it. It's in the lawsuit—$5,000 for the child care Tony did not perform, while recovering from the dinged finger—trebled to $15,000. This would be what Singlaub, Secord, and the other defendants owe Martha Honey for baby-sitting her own kids.

Next, how about $10,000 to Martha—trebled to $30,000—for "loss of consortium" when the dinged finger prevented Tony from being a proper husband to Martha. What a rip!

The rest of the claims are much larger, but less entertaining.

1) For treatment and medical transportation, $125,000. That's for the finger, and, of course, the private Learjet. Avirgan and Honey by no means laid out this amount.
2) Loss of income, $15,000, allegedly a result of being hospitalized for three months, which of course he was not.
3) As for pain and suffering, a nice round million might soothe it away.
4) Punitive damages of $10,000,000 for "generating the overt act" is an even nicer round number.
5) That aforementioned loss of consortium.
6) The baby-sitting charge.
7) Plus $10,000 for mysterious threats Avirgan says he received during the summer of 1984.
8) Plus $25,000 for damage to Honey's more sensitive psyche.
9) And on top of that, $10,000 for security measures.
10) Punitive damages for the threats, and for allegedly "torturing and killing David in order to terrify the plaintiffs," $5,000,000. Imagine— $5 million for something that did not occur!
11) Tony's lost equipment was supposedly worth $60,000 (It had already been paid for by ABC).
12) Loss of income for each of the plaintiffs, $20,000. (Isn't that in there earlier, with a lower figure? Maybe no one will notice.)
13) And finally, $5,000,000 punitive damages for "attempting to intimidate and silence professional journalists . . . in 1985."
    Sheehan's total claim, what with the trebled damages, came to $23,840,000.

Only the government can send you to prison. When Sheehan says, "they're going to . . . get put in jail for the rest of their lives," *he* can't do it because he is not a government prosecutor trying a criminal RICO case. Still, fantasy time involved an amenable administration which would imprison the defendants, after the Christics delivered them all tied up in red ribbon.

Some of the dry stuff consisted of alleged violations of banking laws, the Boland Amendment, the National Security Act, and the Neutrality Act. (President Franklin D. Roosevelt, by the way, spent the better part of 1940 and 1941 violating the Neutrality Act. But don't ever expect to see it mentioned.)

The really juicy charges were items like "terrorist bombings, arson, and murder," pertaining to the bomb at La Penca; "kidnapping" of Carlos Rojas and David; "attempted murder" of the U.S. Ambassador, Lewis Tambs, in a bizarre sub-plot; plus arms and narcotics trafficking, theft, and obstruction of justice.

The alleged plot against Ambassador Tambs has a fatal flaw—timing. Tambs' "movements" in Costa Rica were supposedly under discussion by CIA assassins *four months* before he arrived to take up his duties.

While the La Penca bombing actually occurred—an important consideration in a Sheehan case, where wishes and opinions become fact—Sheehan was simply unable to link his targeted individuals to it.

As for David, he would be happy to announce that he was not kidnapped, tortured, murdered, and buried on John Hull's ranch. But Carlos, who was whisked away to Canada and remains, presumably, wherever the Christics have stashed him, may have that kidnapped feeling by now.

Lewis Tambs does not for one instant credit the Christic charge that CIA minions were going to assassinate him. This, too, rests upon hearsay from the kidnapped-tortured-murdered David, not the walking-around one who looks exactly like him.

The Christics love to sling drug-trafficking charges, too. John Hull is always tagged for having huge shipments staging through the airstrip on his ranch. Convicted pilots will say so. The problem is, the planes they claim to have flown, with loads as stated, simply could not have operated off that strip, according to Hull. It's too short. The laws of physics cannot be bent and broken, unlike the laws of man.

The bottom line is that many of the alleged offenses simply did not occur at all. Thus, *no one* was guilty of them, much less the chosen defendants.

Other offenses may or may not have occurred; Sheehan hasn't proven a thing, however.

The Legal Terrorists' War of Attrition

"They're going to lose everything they have," was Danny Sheehan's boast to his supporters and friends at Piedmont, California, on September 4, 1987.

Sheehan has millions in tax-free dollars with which to fuel his attack. His defendants do not have tax-free assets with which to fight back. At once, Sheehan is on track toward his goal. All he need do is get into court and drag it out.

The Rule 11 penalties assessed by Judge King, in February, 1989, showed the judge's very careful examination of defense costs. The majority of the lesser defendants, including the ones whose names were only intended to lend scuzz to the list, spent nothing.

Of course, the Colombian drug lords could have paid for their defense; they could have paid *everything* out of petty cash. But they were not even served with papers.

The cost of defense was borne by those "major defendants," the people the Christics were really out to get, and as Judge King determined, they either paid or owed their lawyers over a million dollars.

They could not afford to fight, but they were forced to do it. They would lose everything if they did not—and might lose everything, even if they could prove themselves innocent.

That is the idea. Legal terrorists believe in wars of attrition.

Fenton Communications

Sheehan did not trouble himself with such conventional matters as contacting the defendants and/or their lawyers before filing the suit. Nor did he bother to serve papers on them first. This must have been a disappointment to "Father Gumshoe," who gets his jollies by pouncing on luckless Christic defendants.

No, this was to be a media event from the start. Sheehan hired Fenton Communications, a small Washington public-relations firm with a highly-specialized clientele, to stage an extravaganza at the National Press Club.

David Fenton, said to be 37, started out with the "White Panther Party." David Horowitz describes the party program as "rock, drugs, and sex in the streets." Fenton then joined Liberation News Service, which honored and supported the Vietcong.

Next stop, *Rolling Stone,* and his first link-up with the Christics. Fenton helped Sara Nelson raise money for the Silkwood project, and then put together, with Jackson Browne, an anti-nuke musicians' group which adorns letterheads and claims to fame.

Fenton is, or has been, the registered agent of the grubbiest governments around, such as those of Grenada and Angola. David Fenton lost the Sandinista account to a pair of former Maryknoll priests in New York who now sell Danny Ortega for a living. But he got Michael Manley's Jamaica instead.

The firm has also listed Andreas Papandreou's Greek government as a client, as well as Guillermo Ungo, front-man for the Salvadoran FMLN guerrillas, Philip Agee of the Turncoats, Neil Kinnock, reddest of the British labor leaders, and Oliver Tambo, "King of the Necklacers," the African National Congress terrorists who impose their views by burning alive in the street, one by one, some 700 blacks in South Africa. The Christics find themselves in congenial company.

Engineered Hysteria

It was David Fenton who created the Great Apple Hysteria early in 1989. He could not resist boasting of his supremely effective media blitz—a boast reproduced by the *Wall Street Journal* on October 3, 1989.

Losses of at least $100 million were sustained by everyone from apple growers to retailers, as a Fenton barrage of propaganda spread the message, "They're giving our kids cancer with apples!"

Vast quantities of good food were wasted.

Fenton is proud to state that he and his client, the Rockefeller-funded Natural Resource Defense Council, made bags of money on the Alar scare.

Someone then had the brilliant notion of piggy-backing a "hit" on Chile, taking advantage of the panic reaction to Fenton's apple scare. Rumors were spread, and somehow, attention was directed to the two or three grapes among zillions imported from Chile which showed traces of cyanide. Losses and wastage were, once again, enormous.

La Penca: The Ambush

The announcement of the lawsuit was a classic ambush.

Oh, there was one advance leak. Julia Preston, then of the *Boston Globe,* now of the *Washington Post,* was plugged in to the Christics and could not contain herself. She had to call Andy Messing a week ahead of time, but she did not tell him much. She only asked how he liked being sued for $23.8

million.

Andy Messing is certainly ready to call it legal terrorism! The charges were great copy—a huge criminal conspiracy, with lots of lurid ''detail,'' involving those right-wingers they all so love to hate.

David Marash, whose ''Committee to Protect Journalists'' had helped to finance Avirgan and Honey's book, is a Washington TV newscaster. He was at the Press Club to call for solidarity. They owed it to all journalists, he said, to play this one big.

And so the phones began to ring at the homes and offices of the major defendants. Do you know you are being sued for arson, murder, drug-trafficking, gun-running, kidnapping, assault, money-laundering, conspiracy . . .?

Um, actually, no, I didn't.

Well, what have you to say to these charges? You didn't do it? How boring, how predictable, hardly news at all . . .

The personnel of the media are not innocent babes, unaware of why they have been gathered together by Fenton Communications. They were expected to *deliver,* without giving needless thought to the absence of evidence.

The Affidavit and the Witnesses

The same people who have never forgiven Senator Joseph McCarthy for his ''I-have-a-list'' act, find it easy to overlook Sheehan's follow-on. Sheehan marched into federal court with a list of seventy-nine witnesses he said would attest to the veracity of the statements in his sworn affidavit. Unfortunately, he told the judge, he could not reveal their identities, because the defendants were a rough lot, assassins, and his witnesses dwelt in terror.

He got away with this for eight months. Defense lawyers were helpless to refute the anonymous ''testimony'' being trumpeted through the mass media. And, meanwhile, armed with federal subpoena powers, the Christics were allowed to cart away enormous quantities of records belonging to the defendants.

It was Sheehan's fond and desperate hope that, somewhere in these records, he would find actual evidence, before the ludicrous factual basis of his case had to be revealed.

The case is set forth in the famous, or infamous, ''Sheehan affidavit.'' It has appeared in various editions. The first was tossed back to Sheehan by Judge King, who recommended that he visit a law library. The latest edition is dated July, 1988, and is sold by the Christics in book form, under the title

Inside the Shadow Government.

An intermediate version was the basis of Christic Comix, as well as Leslie Cockburn's book, *Out of Control,* and her procession of television specials. The spreading stain of Sheehan's charges is shown in greater detail in the section on the media.

As previous experience with the Silkwood episode illustrates, Sheehan can rank as a major myth-maker, so long as he can rely upon enthusiastic support, uncritical acceptance, or discreet silence from the mass media. Critical exposure is what is needed, but that is not what he receives.

The author's crude legal education began with a snap comment from a leading defendant, "Books aren't evidence." The subject arose because the Sheehan affidavit is a pastiche of material culled from the deluge of books which the Vietnam War engendered.

Said education then involved a harsh apprenticeship indeed—the job of reading "the Wheaton deposition." This is cited hundreds of times by Sheehan in *Inside the Shadow Government.* The thing is over one thousand pages long, representing about two weeks of maundering testimony and legal squabbling. But it was a major lesson. The Wheaton deposition is one hundred percent hearsay.

Eventually, the defense lawyers get a crack at Mr. Wheaton. At which point we learn that Mr. Wheaton, a smug but nervous gentleman, is a down-and-out former warrant officer who tried but failed to obtain a piece of the action in supplying the contras, and bears a grudge against Richard Secord. Wheaton's background needed considerable padding-out with styrofoam to become that of an authority and expert.

Evidently, Wheaton heard through the grapevine that Sheehan was in the market for information. What Wheaton had was fragmentary hearsay, but nothing that could not be fleshed out by the Sheehan imagination. Much of the "Iranian venture" of the "racketeering enterprise" described in agonizing detail in the famous affidavit was built upon the sands of what Eugene Wheaton says he heard somebody say to someone else about yet another party, in Iran in 1976 . . .

In retrospect, too, it would appear that some of Sheehan's own grapevine-gleanings from Silkwood days were mysteriously transferred to Mr. Wheaton's brain, thenceforth to issue from Mr. Wheaton's mouth as testimony.

For example, incoherent comments on the subject of Andros Island, in the Bahamas, which appear in *The Killing of Karen Silkwood,* published before La Penca was even a gleam in Sheehan's eye, reappear in expanded form in the Wheaton deposition. The trouble is, the spooky installations and murderous activities referred to find no other confirmation. Ever. Anywhere.

But who is to know that? The entry-level reader is snowed blind, figuring, "But my goodness, this is a legal document, a sworn affidavit by a lawyer, and here is a witness giving direct sworn testimony, so I guess it must be true."

All this testimony must be smoothed and tidied, and if necessary deodorized, before becoming a docudrama and a major motion picture. The affidavit, in its various editions, has seen the holes chinked in and the rough spots sanded down.

No doubt Daniel Sheehan wishes that Mr. Wheaton had not mentioned the part about being paid $20,000 in small bills for his services, however described, to the Christic Institute, but you will not find that aspect cited in *Inside the Shadow Government.*

Nor will the reader learn from the Christics that the Institute is not merely a source of free legal services, but it will actually pay its plaintiffs, if the propaganda payoff is high enough. Avirgan and Honey have been receiving $50,000 a year from the Christics. The Christics slipped once, and allowed that to appear on their IRS Form 990. It is smarter to leave it buried within the big round numbers for "investigation" and "litigation."

Other cited witnesses, once Sheehan was required to reveal them, could not believe it happened. He had promised he would not. Carl Jenkins testified, "I am astounded that on the basis of his conversations with me Mr. Sheehan would swear under oath that I supplied him with *any* of this information." He added that lawyer Sheehan "said to me that he was not concerned with the actual state of my knowledge, and that he was using the affidavit simply to keep the case in court, so that he could take discovery."

Sheehan's "Source #72" had no idea of his role until contacted by the defense, when he said, "I find it amazing that [Sheehan] would represent to a court that I have personal knowledge concerning his ridiculous accusations."

As the author summarized matters in the September/October 1989 issue of *Chief Executive* magazine,

> Once Judge King forced Sheehan to surface his witnesses, the effect was much like turning over a rock. Some scuttled for cover, while others blinked into the unaccustomed light with a "Who, me?" expression. Some were dead, some unidentifiable. At least half a dozen had led "double lives." That is, Source #24 could

corroborate Source #48, since they were one and the same. An absolutely key witness turned out to be someone named David, in Costa Rica. That's it!

Sheehan's wish-list of *trial* witnesses numbered 2,176, twelve percent of whom were dead at the time. But clearly, he looked forward to the Trial of the Century.

What we have here is a bad case of "let's pretend." Maybe bluff *is* a big item in a lawyer's bag of tricks, but the lawyer is supposed to keep a cool head about his own wish-fulfillment dreams, and it does not appear that Sheehan is able to do so.

Let us entertain the idea that Sheehan is not really as bemused by his own yarn as all that. Suppose that he simply wants to gain control of the records of the defendants, because he, and others, are quite interested in their contents, and not necessarily for purposes of the lawsuit.

Jack Singlaub was head of the World Anti-Communist League, which Sheehan purports to view as a bunch of goons, illegally countering Communist plans for social change and a rosy tomorrow. If we are talking wish-fulfillment, the Communists would very much like to know the most intimate details of what Jack Singlaub has been doing, and stop him from doing it.

Sheehan has come closer than anyone to accomplishing that. Will Sheehan protect Jack Singlaub's private papers from intrusive gaze? On his record, would you bet on that proposition? The author asked defense attorney Thomas Spencer what was to prevent Sheehan and the Christics from turning over material to the KGB and was told, "Nothing."

In a very interesting passage in the court record, we find Sheehan complaining that Jack Singlaub's check stubs—in the possession of the Christic Institute, you understand—"indicate he also has a program to aid the 'freedom fighters' of Afghanistan. Plaintiffs have not been allowed discovery in this matter—. . . [but] Defendant Singlaub and the Enterprise of which he is part continue to be involved in criminal racketeering activity."

Let's pick this apart and examine it more closely. Judge King had tried to confine discovery to a four-year period bracketing the La Penca bombing, in a futile effort to keep Sheehan's mind on the case, rather than the writing of revisionist history.

Afghanistan is one long way from La Penca. If the plaintiffs and their attorney were simply seeking to gain compensation, and penalize malefactors, they would be concentrating upon the task at hand—trying to prove that the defendants were responsible for the bombing at La Penca.

But, instead, Sheehan is digging for intel on the Afghan resistance. Does this tell us something about his motives?

CHAPTER SIX

THE ROLE OF THE MASS MEDIA

As we have seen with the Silkwood case, the Davis-Sheehan-Nelson *modus operandi* is the two-pronged assault. The proverbial "federal case" is only one half. The other half is the "public opinion" battle.

And, as in the case of Silkwood, even failure in the courtroom can still leave a public-opinion victory.

The Silkwood grand conspiracy and murder theory went nowhere in court. But the theory has been inserted into "what we think we know" about the Silkwood case, simply by the work of sympathizers in the mass media.

A motion picture which, in effect, straddles the ground between the court record and Sheehan's yarns makes a much better story, with lots more drama. Without actually lying, those creating the film are enabled to satisfy a certain "constituency."

The looming headlights at the end *imply* that Silkwood was run off the road, when there is no evidence for this whatsoever. The film *leaves the impression* that Silkwood was murdered by her greedy corporate employer, although the film never says this.

This is called "docudrama," and represents *dezinformatsiya,* American style. Kerr-McGee gave up, when faced with it.

Anyone who does not believe a movie could be made from the Christics' La Penca case simply lacks imagination. Christic Comix is halfway there.

Winning in court would be both gratifying and extremely profitable, but even *losing* is hardly a disaster. It, too, can be profitable in terms of money and propaganda.

What of the supposedly serious working press, as distinct from the enter-tainment and "docudrama" crowd?

John Barron, a journalist of long experience, now Senior Editor of *Reader's Digest*, offered some very succinct comments on the role of the press in the La Penca case.

He found it "dismaying," to say the least, that people could be pilloried and financially drained in this manner, with what amounts to the collaboration of the press.

He ticked off his points as follows:

1) "the failure of the press to seek comment from reputable people who have been accused of crimes."

2) "the failure of prestigious publications to inquire as to the evidence justifying the charges."

3) "as the case proceeded and deposition evidence became avail-able, the failure to report that some witnesses were non-existent, or repudiated the testimony attributed to them."

4) "after dismissal of the case, press stories continued to suggest that it had a basis, when the judge found that it did not."

In sum, he concluded that "customary standards have been abandoned, to the great harm of people thus far found innocent."

Barron's statement was measured and devastating, if we are talking about the customary and traditional rules of fair play in journalism. However, "advocacy journalism" throws out the old rules and brings everybody down a notch.

The *New York Times,* the grey lady of supposed respectability, the flagship of American print journalism, should never be forgiven for its role in mobi-lizing American support for Fidel Castro, in the late 1950s. It permitted a leftist editor, Herbert Matthews, whose proclivities had been worn on his sleeve since the Spanish Civil War of the 1930s, to lie outright on behalf of Castro—for years!

The rest of the American press dutifully trailed behind in the dust, accepting the party line from the *Times*. There were exceptions, publications crying in the wilderness, "but Castro is a Communist!" They were reviled, ignored, marginalized, and silenced by the power of the "prestige press."

The consequences have been enormous—for all Cubans, for all Ameri-cans, and for the balance of power in the hemisphere and the world. If the error had been recognized and regretted, perhaps we would not have seen a replay exactly thirty years later, on behalf of the Sandinistas. But, since it *was* repeated, perhaps these episodes are not errors at all.

This is merely one egregious example of the power of the left, in the American press.

The *Times,* let it be said, behaved with more caution with respect to the Christic case, occasionally finding fault with Sheehan's "evidentiary thread," and only giving the story ink when it could no longer resist the Christic sandbagging. But the *Times* has made no effort to report what the defendants have to say.

The leftist bias of the American media as a whole has been proven "scientifically" in the 1985 Lichter-Rothman survey of attitudes of some 3000 American reporters and editors. A 1987 Gallup poll, which received understandably little publicity, demonstrated a falling-off in public confidence in the media. Eighty percent of Americans thought the presentation of news to be biased, and two-to-one, they thought it to be biased toward the left, not the right.

The *Washington Post* is notorious for both docudrama and fiction (speaking of Bob Woodward and Janet Cook), and for its overwhelmingly pro-Sandinista coverage of Nicaragua, for example.

And the recent boasting of a Marxist mole, who twits the *Los Angeles Times* and the *Wall Street Journal* for ignoring his biased reportage, is particularly instructive. A. Kent MacDougall has been given a safe perch as a professor of journalism at Berkeley, there to be supported by the California taxpayers as he boasts of his deceptions and tells students how to follow in his footsteps. He says his work was "usually covert."

Everything depends upon whose covert action it is.

Accuracy in Media devoted a four-page issue to MacDougall in January of 1989. In fact, MacDougall's own article, describing how he slipped Marxist "truths" past supposedly wise and objective editors, should be an eye-opener to readers, even as it serves as a career guide to MacDougall's students.

After all, MacDougall's subversive work could not have been overly subtle, or he would never have made his points to his readers. That readers can be more discerning than biased or blind-eyed editors is demonstrated by *Accuracy in Media,* which shows that letters from readers, making that precise point, were joked over by MacDougall and his editors and filed with the "crank mail."

Readers *were* correct, MacDougall *was* a mole, and his editors were fools or worse. This is just one example of what can be multiplied thousands of times, except that the confession is lacking. The fact is that the left consistently benefits from the uncritical or self-blinded members of the press corps.

How odd to find an apt rumination at the tail end of Gerry Spence's book, *Gunning for Justice.* Speaking of the mass media, he says:

> These new gunmen shielded themselves with the First Amend-
> ment, which gave them freedom even to defame innocent people
> so long as the defamed person couldn't prove the media had been
> malicious or reckless. That was the holding, in part, of the U.S.
> Supreme Court in *New York Times vs Sullivan.*
>
> These new gunfighters didn't need the old gunfighters' quick
> hand and stout nerves, coming face to face with adversaries who
> could shoot back. Instead, they could spew their word-bullets out
> on the countryside, killing our leaders with libels, killing our
> statesmen and our heroes. They have killed most of them with
> impunity, hidden behind the First Amendment.

When it comes to pushing the leftist line, the film and television industry are exceedingly cooperative. The Christics have learned, from previous experience, what they can expect.

Any number of entertainers support the Christics although no one can match Jackson Browne for dollars delivered. Father Davis is happy to say that Jane Fonda and Ed Asner have been "very supportive." Other entertainment figures adorn Christic fundraisers and circulate at the wine-and-cheese parties.

Father Davis must have found gratification in Costa-Gavras' *Missing.* And, as Cliff Kincaid pointed out to the author, Davis, Sheehan, and Nelson can feel great personal gratification about the films *Silkwood, Lethal Weapon, Above the Law,* and *Coverup* (the latter a cult rather than popular flick). Their propaganda has been inserted, as obviously as possible, into a season finale of *Miami Vice,* and an episode of *Cagney and Lacey* in which a lead character says, "Danny Sheehan is my hero."

Leslie Cockburn was able to deliver for the Christics three times on CBS commercial channels. Christic Comix cites as "sources" her three "West 57th Street" productions, *John Hull's Farm Bordering on War,* June 25, 1986; *The CIA Connection: Drugs for Guns,* April 6, 1987; and *CIA Front Dealing Drugs,* July 11, 1987.

One could hardly say that the Columbia Broadcasting System has not been cooperative!

But "your tax dollars are also at work." Public television has not been far behind. PBS aired Bill Moyers' *The Secret Government: The Constitution in Crisis* on November 4, 1987. The show was jazzed up with snippets of a Jackson Browne propaganda video, and a succession of speakers from Philip Agee's Turncoat Brigade.

PBS also gave the husband-wife team of Leslie and Andrew Cockburn free rein, on May 17, 1988, for their predictable opus, *Guns, Drugs, & the CIA.*

Yet another Christic "coup" is Ms. Cockburn's translation of Daniel Sheehan's "sworn affidavit" into *Out of Control,* which *Atlantic Monthly* is pleased to call a book—although it lacks even a table of contents, much less an index. It was simply a rush job, to help out the Christics.

When Cliff Kincaid debated Sheehan in late November 1987, he was confronted by callers all agog, just having seen Moyers' show, or running on about the Cockburn book. Sheehan bit his tongue so as not to take credit for all of it, since it was smarter to let the public think there is all this independent confirmation!

This kind of "self-generated verification" is a standard Soviet disinformation technique.

The traditional occupation of the Cockburn family is that of Communist propagandist. *Pere* Claud Cockburn served in that capacity in the Spanish Civil War, churning out fictional atrocity stories to order. Although he parted formal company with the Party *apparat* later in life, he never ceased to serve the Marxist cause. Sons Alexander and Andrew have their varied specialties, and Andrew's wife Leslie encounters no difficulty in adapting to family habits.

The extent to which the American media are both wittingly and unwittingly manipulated by the left is impossible to overestimate. Big, big bucks from leftist foundations make possible large-scale deception and professional disinformation.

An examination of the grants of these foundations presage what you will see on television half a year or a year down the line. These campaigns are planned in detail by professionals, and lay out a party line. The topics may seem unrelated, but they maintain common objectives—demoralization, disunity, de-industrialization, reduced military strength, throttling regulation, and unproductive expenditure.

With only the Christics as an example, we have demonstrated the way in which a fraudulent lawsuit has been spread world-wide, repeated, amplified, embroidered and caused to become both mythology and public record. The defendants, who do not command the sympathies of the media and entertainment world, have no chance whatever of countering the injustices inflicted upon them by this libelous barrage.

The Christics can declare victory in the propaganda war.

CHAPTER SEVEN

LA PENCA: THE MONEY-MINE

The Christics literally struck gold with the La Penca lawsuit. They have doubled and redoubled their income with it.

"Soaking It Up" was the title of Alex Cockburn's intriguing two-pager in *Nation* magazine, May 29, 1989. The Christics' staggering haul of $2.6 million in 1988, on the basis of the La Penca case alone, has teed off the rest of the hardscrabble left, enough so to have Cockburn turn on his sister-in-law's own favorite cause.

"These days," snorts Cockburn, "when people round the country ask me what I think of the Christic Institute, I piss on them just a little harder than I used to . . . [W]hat irks me most is that whatever the ups and downs—now mostly downs—in its fortunes, the Christic Institute trundles along with undiminished energy in the activity at which it has without doubt been most successful: namely, raising money for itself.

". . . Meanwhile, there are important campaigns, magazines, and information centers on the left dying for want of a few hundred or thousand dollars. Many times I have heard people from such outfits say with exasperation and understandable envy that Christic has soaked up a large quantity of the finite amount of cash that all the usual bankrollers of good causes are prepared to dish out."

Cause indeed for grumbling among the reds and passion pinks of America, and it may be the only silver lining to this whole thing for the defendants. Look, here they are, patriotically absorbing, as salvos of slander and libel, the financial resources which would otherwise be spread like green manure over Cockburn's favorite charities, which include the needy *Nation* itself.

Cockburn points out some other examples. There is *Shmate,* "journal of progressive Jewish thought," trying to stay above water by appealing to the prurient interests of its sadly limited readership. How about this? "A searching interview with sex film actress Nina Hartley [star of some 170 porn flicks], and feminist socialist." A chat with an ideologically-correct sexpot—what more can be asked?

Starved for the money going to the Christics, we find old socialist Paul Sweezy. For forty years, he has been writing books about the demise of capitalism and the great dawn of the socialist era. He has lived through all seventy-two years of that great dawn, kicking his way across the litter of bleached bones and corpses set in permafrost in the killing-fields of Communism without ever glancing down.

Cockburn: How do you think Mao looks these days?

Sweezy: I think he looks great. . . . he really inspired people to believe [the things] which have to be done to have a decent society.

I haven't seen anything in Marx that isn't good . . . He's got better and better. Mao is the only real Marxist . . .

"Send them a huge check," Cockburn advises, because Sweezy discusses the problems "in a language we can share."

This doesn't call for green manure. This calls for quicklime.

The Christics certainly do not advertise the identity of their money-cows. This might well be considered proprietary information. The foundations, the churches, the Hollywood crowd—all information must be winkled out as if from caves.

"Thou shalt not bear false witness?" Try that on the church bureaucrats and hierarchs who, wittingly or not, have paid the plaintiffs and paid the witnesses.

And then there is the entertainment world, where Causes may be dead serious, or they may be no more than today's latest fad in Concerns, worn like jewelry. But the money! Oh, the money!

Look at the overall income of the Institute from the beginning. Calendar 1981 showed a take of $257,000—and an alarming drop-off to $193,000 in 1982. Clearly, it was up to Sara Nelson to pick up the pace, or they were all going to have to find jobs. So 1983 reflected her determined efforts with a haul of $559,000. Then there was a pre-La Penca plateau level of about $740,000 in 1984 and 1985.

The La Penca media splash occurred at the end of May, 1986, and did not manifest itself in any great surge of money that year; the propaganda blitz bore fruit in 1987, when income doubled—and then soared, in 1988, to a record $2,622,000, despite the blow of summary judgment for the defendants in July of 1988. What this suggests, reflecting upon both 1986 and 1988, is that the rush of funds comes in the first half of the year, and is thus little affected by events later in that year.

It will be interesting to see the 1989 harvest of dollars. The desperate collection of $1.2 million to cover the Rule 11 penalties will weigh in, but will there be any signs of disillusionment, as well? Sara Nelson may have her work cut out for her, as the Christics have had all their eggs in the La Penca basket for some time now.

Having had the case thrown out of court is not a fact the Christics were in any rush to advertise. The press—to the great disservice of the long-suffering defendants—barely mentioned it at all, and it is silly to ask whether the media responded with a tide of exposés, instant books, docudramas, or TV specials taking apart the Christic claims. They did not. There were, of course, a few articles in periodicals of both radical and conservative outlook, and there was some commentary in legal journals, but this was far from balancing the scales of justice.

Welcome to a Christic Fundraiser

The author attended a fundraiser at the Warner Theater in Washington, D.C. on January 19, 1989. The program involved possible hearing loss, as the tactic seems to be to make up in decibels what is missing in talent, and blast the audience out the rear wall in the equivalent of an auditory thrill-ride.

Prior to departure, the author asked for comments from the younger generation, and learned the following. Re: "Bobcat" Goldthwaite, "He's nuts!" and re: David Crosby, "That old man?"

Goldthwaite is an unfunny comedian whose *shtick* is a slob act. There is a great deal of flying spittle, and a bath towel is employed ostentatiously in mopping sweat, to show how hard he is trying.

Later, given the opportunity to speak to Goldthwaite, the author remained at a cautious distance until it became clear that Goldthwaite does not spit, in ordinary conversation. He was, in fact, restoring lost bodily fluids, but had time to lay out his complaints.

He found his New York audiences "frightening," with "Morton Downey jeering," but this was as nothing compared to the South, where his reception was "terrifying."

"I can't do my work," he wailed, expecting sympathy. He might ask Sheehan to establish the Constitutional right of unfunny comedians to a friendly reception, on First Amendment grounds.

David Crosby of the vaunted "Woodstock generation" appeared quite ancient. Stringy white hair cascaded from pate to shoulders, and he carried a load of blubber sufficient to produce a matronly bosom. Portions of his anatomy mooned through threadbare trousers.

Sapping morale, the author moved around, commenting softly, "The years have not been kind to David Crosby," and hearing a litany of his "problems" with drugs, jail, and so on.

Then there was a discussion of the Altamont benefit concert of about twenty years ago. Gee, Mr. Crosby, remember how the Hell's Angels were used for security, because the real cops were to be despised? Remember how the Angels beat up on everybody, and even killed one fan, while the rest of the crowd grooved on the scene?

Crosby grew ever more uncomfortable as the author ran on, reminding him about when drummer Marty Balin tried to save some fan, and the Angels beat him as well. Just think—a percussion improvisation on Marty Balin's head, and it was neither amplified nor recorded. Crosby couldn't recall a thing; he said he was zonked on drugs at the time.

How sad, to have your glory days a blank.

Does it help, trying to lay the blame on the "secret team?" Or does David Crosby have few calls upon his talent nowadays?

Kris Kristofferson was the big draw, and was a physically fit contrast to Crosby, although he may be overdoing the exercise—piling muscle on a naturally slight build, looking drawn rather than merely lean.

The topic of discussion was the TV series "Amerika." This was aired in 1987, in belated response to the earlier ABC "surrender now" series entitled "The Day After." Kristofferson was chosen to star in a silly story about America under Soviet occupation. The nature of a Soviet occupation is perfectly well documented, and the show bore little resemblance to actual experience endured by occupied peoples.

Kristofferson said little new. He was already on record as having taken the part to prevent "some right-winger" from having it, and having rushed to Moscow to apologize in person for any aspersions he may have cast upon the benevolence of Soviet conquest and occupation policies! He added that he had been instrumental in removing some "conservative propaganda that was anti-UN and anti-Soviet,'' and dropped a bit of news by saying that he had tried to alter the script so that it would tell the audience that we had been conquered by the Soviets because we *deserved* to be conquered, having "alienated the Third World and all our allies.'' In other words, America the Loathsome deserved its fate. Evidently, even ABC thought that was a little raw.

Thus we end our interviews with entertainers supporting the La Penca lawsuit.

The event was covered only by the *Guardian*. The author chatted with *Guardian* reporter Jack Colhoun, who still could not decide whether he had deserted from the U.S. Army, or had merely gone AWOL for eight years. As in the case of Avirgan, the government never held such misbehavior against him.

The Christics maintain a Los Angeles office which taps the wealth of the Hollywood left. If these gilded coke-snorters really believed the Christic *spiel,* they would hang their heads and kick the habit because they had been supporting the contras all this time, and financing nefarious CIA plots. But, of course, they believe none of it and do neither.

And so, let us leave Father Davis passing the collection plate in Cocaine Canyon.

"A" is for Anagnos, and also for "Angel"

The Christics could not ask for a more generous sugar-daddy than Aris Anagnos. When it became necessary for the Christic Institute to put up the $1,200,000 required by the federal court under Rule 11 sanctions, Aris Anagnos provided half of that, which he will lose if Sheehan's appeal fails, and the victims of the Christics receive at least partial compensation for the enormous expense to which Danny Sheehan has put them.

The Anagnos treasure-chest had funded the Christics previously. The extent to which it had done so is not known, because neither the Christics nor the Anagnos family have any desire to impart this information to outsiders. However, it has been said that by mid-1987, Aris and Carolyn Anagnos had helped to raise $50,000 for the Christics from their circle of friends.

Aris Anagnos arrived in America from Greece at the age of 23, soon after World War II, and attended the University of California at Los Angeles. His wife, the former Carolyn Williams, is a Berkeley product with a degree in political science, with results which do not require a great deal of imagination. It would be interesting to know whether Aris, Carolyn, or both of them became acquainted with Andreas Papandreou during his lengthy tenure as an economics professor at Berkeley in the 1950s.

Papandreou was known as a Marxist in pre-war Greece. He, like Anagnos, came to the United States as a young man; he became an American citizen and served in the U.S. Navy during World War II. Then he attended Harvard and became a professor of economics. Whether he described himself as a Marxist or a socialist at the time is probably irrelevant. By 1959, the Ford and Rockefeller Foundations were so enamored of his work that he was able to spend five years with one foot in Berkeley and the other in Athens, where he headed the Economic Research Center. At that time, his father, George "the Fox" Papandreou, was moving along toward becoming Prime Minister.

Andreas became a member of the Greek parliament, and his father then placed him in charge of the Greek equivalent of the CIA, the KYP. He lost no time in purging non-Marxists, and initiated the notorious *Aspida* conspiracy, which aimed to end the constitutional monarchy, pull Greece out of NATO, and establish a Marxist dictatorship. Years later, Andreas Papandreou would become a "socialist" Prime Minister of Greece in his own right, presiding over a resurgence of Communist strength in Greece. He also has been suspected of involvement in the plundering of the Bank of Crete for hundreds of millions of *dollars,* not *drachmae.* Just what happened to all this money is something the new Greek government will examine.

This is not an idle aside, because Prime Minister Andreas Papandreou made Aris Anagnos (*nee* Aristides Anagnostopoulos) the honorary Greek Consul in Los Angeles—and threw the Greek public relations account to the notoriously leftist Fenton Communications outfit, the one which represents the dregs of the Third World Communist countries—plus the Christics.

That someone, entering the insurance and real estate business in Los Angeles in the 1950s, made a fortune for himself is not particularly surprising. It is the readiness with which Anagnos hands off hundreds of thousands of dollars, with little hope of ever seeing a financial return, which arouses curiosity. He seems content to settle for a political and ideological return. The Anagnos' have other expensive political tastes besides the Christics. They have been pillars of the left wing of the Democratic Party of California, and also of the Southern California branch of the American Civil Liberties Union, which even the ACLU considers a tad radical in outlook. Their daughter is or was a power in that group.

In line with the Anagnos' left-wing interests, they have inserted themselves into the conduct of U.S. foreign policy in Central America. Aris Anagnos apparently went to El Salvador in 1985 to meet leaders of the Communist guerrillas, and returned with the message that we ought to allow them to take that country.

In 1986, along with Americans for Democratic Action, he initiated a lawsuit intended to prevent the California Air National Guard from training in Panama. A similar measure was pressed in Dukakis-governed Massachusetts. This was part of a nationwide campaign to prevent the deployment of Guard units to any part of Central America for training. The well-known if unspoken aspect of that deployment was to remind all parties that the United States does have military strength, and a few options along those lines. It was meant to stiffen the backbones of friendly governments as well as to send a warning to hostile governments and guerrilla forces. The campaign to block guard training was intended to send a different message—that our military strength can be neutralized and paralyzed by powerful leftist opposition in the United States.

In 1988, Aris Anagnos "generously" spent $50,000 to retrieve from Nicaragua an American whose private plane was brought down there. Jim Denby was accused of being a CIA agent, but was released as part of a deal to block the granting of further U.S. aid to the contras by Congress.

The Christics have an office at 8773 Venice Blvd., Los Angeles; its function is largely to shake out contributions, and its existence might be justified by stroking the Anagnos family alone. But, as Christic donor Peg Yorkin noted, "This is the Gold Coast. This is where the money is."

Foundation Support

The following is a necessarily incomplete summary of non-religious, tax-exempt funding sources of the Christics. Clearly, non-cooperation has been the rule. Some few foundations do answer questions readily, but many others stonewall or reveal a certain surly resentment of inquiries. The Foundation Centers in various large cities are gold-mines for the very patient digger, however.

For many of the foundations which support the Christic Institute, the key word is "networking." They exist to nurture and knit together into an effective weapon for "social change" a vast array of "groups," however tiny. Three people and a dog can be the Institute of This and also the Center for That, and if the Cause is leftist, they need never fear that their actual insignificance will be exposed.

In William Poole's excellent study of the so-called Youth Project, of

Washington, D.C., it is clearly demonstrated that the "Project" sees its function as bringing together like-minded individuals and their "groups" meeting the ideological standards of the hard-eyed left. If they pass muster, they may find themselves maintained in business. If they don't, then they can flounder and sink. That is, the Youth Project aims to become the center of a large network of controlled subsidiary groups, just as the Institute for Policy Studies contrived to do.

"We also support the development of coalitions toward the goal of building broad national constituencies for change." There is no need to ask what kind of change, as these people have in mind anything from supposedly middle-of-the-road, death-by-boredom, extinction-by-birth-control Swedish socialism to the North Korean brand of zombie Communism.

It is instructive to see how foundation programs to "educate" journalists, or people in the entertainment world, are baldly advertised. The objective is to program those who are in a position to influence a larger public. After all, we now sport several generations of "youths" who have been taught to accept policy judgments by entertainment figures lacking a shred of competence, much less expertise.

One need only read the list of grants made by a certain constellation of foundations and funds to understand far more clearly why the network newscasts and Public Broadcasting "documentaries" have certain theme songs. They are "telegraphed" perhaps a year in advance by the foundation grants supporting the creation of the relevant professional propaganda.

In foreign affairs, the semi-permanent targets are those in Communist sights—South Africa, Chile, the Philippines, South Korea, El Salvador . . .

The "concerns" resolve into waves of group-think, and cluster around certain themes, such as the de-industrialization and/or disarmament of the United States, and its socialization. The rule of thumb is this: the left will support anything which weakens America.

The special, leftist-oriented constellation of grant-making bodies—foundations, funds, and funding exchanges—is best represented in an intriguing volume entitled *The Grant Seeker's Guide*. What is intriguing about it is that, once a researcher experiences the vast sea of hundreds of thousands of groups with tax-exempt status, or the tens of thousands of such groups shoveling out substantial sums of money, one comes to realize that this is a rather specialized "guide."

An organization of Christic orientation can go through the book and feel confident of "scoring off" a high percentage of grant-making groups. Most of the following are among them.

Boehm Foundation

They don't like to answer questions. Robert Boehm, rumored to be an "investment banker," is the same Robert Boehm who desires to be de-gendered into chairperson of the Board of the Center for Constitutional Rights, the money-receptacle for radical lawyer William Kunstler, who won Gregory Johnson the right to publicly defile the flag. The Boehm Foundation may also have a link to the Rubin Foundation (see below). Did the Boehm Foundation give to the Christics? They would rather not say. The Center for Constitutional Rights itself responds similarly to inquiries—who are you, why do you want to know anything whatsoever, give us your name and phone number. The Christics say that they received money from the Boehm Foundation, but will not reveal the amount. The Christics have joined Kunstler in many legal battles, including the "flag-burning" case.

Bread and Roses Community Fund

The phrase "bread and roses" evidently derives from an old "labor" song; thus, a surprising number of big-city phone book entries involve Bread and Roses. In search of this fund, it is possible to dial into a gift shop, a vegetarian-food shop, or an abortion clinic before finding the place you want. Philadelphia's Bread and Roses Community Fund gave the Christics $11,500, according to its records.

Bydale Foundation

This one operates out of a law office on Park Avenue, in New York City, and does not appear to be overly generous any more—even though dispensing Warburg money. The Warburg family of merchant bankers goes back a long way. Members of the family had a great deal to do with financing both sides, during World War I. One or both branches funded Lenin's return to Russia in 1917, and the rest is history, as they say. During and after World War II, James P. Warburg was quite insistent that there *would* be a world government. Enthusiasts of world government tend to fall into two classes. The first consists of naive, well-intentioned souls who have not thought this through, and the second consists of people who believe they have some realistic expectation of running a world government. People at the top levels of the financial world often entertain this idea, and Mr. Warburg was among them. Bydale has long financed the Institute for Policy Studies and its spinoff groups. Bydale gave to the Christics early. Whether it gave often is a question the Foundation chooses not to answer.

The Funding Exchange

The Communist *Guardian,* on March 22, 1989, tells a story which is quite heartwarming, from the Communist point of view:

> In the early 1970's, a number of young people who had inherited money but did not want to be involved in traditional philanthropy formed 1960s-style grant-making institutions. George Pillsbury formed the Haymarket Fund in Boston, Sarah Pillsbury started the Liberty Hill Foundation in Los Angeles . . .

The article goes on to include the Vanguard Public Foundation and brings them all together in the Funding Exchange.

> In fiscal 1988, the Funding Exchange distributed $3.2 million to nearly 500 groups . . . In addition, each of 15 [associated] regional foundations gave away between $50,000 and $1 million.

The listing of causes, all receiving Communist approval, is extensive— and includes the *Guardian* itself, which is permanently in need of more money than it can possibly earn through readership. The Funding Exchange, the *Guardian* explains, brought us the Gay and Lesbian march on Washington in 1987, and "has made lesbian and gay concerns a high priority." But this does not mean that they could not spare a dime for the Christics, who are also their kind of people. The Funding Exchange did give, but they are mum on how much, and when.

What we are seeing here is the sad story of the feckless and witless heirs of American capitalism turning over their inheritance to Communists and their allies, to be used in the studied subversion of the United States.

The Max and Anna Levinson Foundation

This foundation, formerly a New York entity and now ensconced in the pleasanter climes of Santa Fe, New Mexico, helped Dan Sheehan to honor himself with a big awards ceremony. It then followed with $30,000 in loans, which were later converted to gifts. The Levinsons are charter donors from Silkwood days.

106

J. Roderick MacArthur Foundation

Although not to be confused with the MacArthur Foundation in Chicago, which has truly staggering assets, this extremely well-heeled foundation has poured money upon the Christics in a steady cascade—averaging over $40,000 per year! The magic words are not unusual. To protect rights, to challenge abuses, to defend civil liberties. . . Annual grants have been between $1.8 and $3.6 million, during 1985 through 1988, on projects ranging from Establishment Liberal to distinctly Red. They have not been spotted funding anything remotely conservative.

Mott Money

Charles Stewart Mott, of General Motors fame, was an American capitalist who would be appalled at what is being done with the fortune he left behind—and which grew and grew, despite the unproductive and anti-productive activities of certain heirs.

The Charles Stewart Mott Foundation, occupying the Mott Building in Flint, Michigan, has enormous assets, and devotes much of them to the support of leftist causes. But this foundation is not so single-minded as that of General Motors heir Stewart J. Mott. His foundation, based in New York City, has been a pillar of support for the radical Institute for Policy Studies and its innumerable spinoffs—for details, see S. Stephen Powell's *Covert Cadre*. Mott has provided sustenance for a great variety of Marxist enterprises even outside of that IPS network.

The Christic Institute could be considered an element of that network nowadays, even though its period of prominence, thanks to the La Penca suit, arrived after Powell's research had ended. The Christics have received relatively modest sums from Stewart Mott—we find record of only $10,000, which is peanuts—but they have done better with Maryanne Mott, proprietor of the C.S. (presumably for Charles Stewart) Fund in California. The C.S. Fund is another rich and enthusiastic member of the constellation of foundations supporting the radical left in the United States. It links itself to the Tides Foundation (see Reynolds Money) and the Youth Project.

Maryanne Mott is mentioned as a charter donor to the Davis-Sheehan-Nelson trio, since Silkwood days. In three years, 1986 to 1988, the C.S. Foundation gave the Christics $100,000, "in support of the Institute's prosecution of the La Penca lawsuit which challenges racketeering and drug trade in conjunction with the war in Central America."

New-Land Foundation

This represents Buttinger family money, although the Buttinger name has died out now in Foundation records. It is a family of wealthy Austrian socialists. In the early days of U.S. involvement in Vietnam, Joseph Buttinger was very interested in the country, an interest reflected in his book *The Lesser Dragon*. He thought he saw an opportunity to convert Vietnam into a society more to liberal and socialist liking. However, with Joseph, and then Muriel Buttinger gone, it is quite possible that New-Land supports the Christics for reasons closer to home, unconnected to the Christic interpretation of events in Vietnam.

The New World Foundation

There seems nothing particularly distinctive about this one. It is part of the nexus funding the Institute for Policy Studies and its satellites, and it has given at least $18,000 to the Christics, apparently recognizing them as ideological clones.

Norman Foundation

Various magic words may draw grants from the Norman Foundation. Its dispensers of largesse bite on keywords like Women's, Citizen's, Worker's, or Children's whatever. The Christics, in the form of the Greensboro Civil Rights Fund, received $5,000 in 1985. Then, as Christics, the Norman Foundation donated $10,000 in 1986 and $15,000 in 1987. The Christics do not appear on the 1988 list of recipients, however.

The Philadelphia Fund

This one has been twitted about "money-laundering," since it asserts, in its literature, that its interests are confined to metropolitan Philadelphia, yet sums have been passed to the Christics. No one will say how much. It seems that donors who wished to remain anonymous gave money to this fund, with orders to run it through the Fund's machinery and thence to the Christics.

Reynolds Money

Richard Joshua Reynolds struck it rich in 1913, when he invented Camels and sold his cigarettes for ten cents a pack instead of the usual fifteen cents. Clearly, like any businessman, he did far more than this to build an enormous and prosperous business. The rise and fall of the Reynolds clan can be followed in the recent book, *The Gilded Leaf,* by Patrick Reynolds, one of the (relatively) disinherited heirs, and one who is currently expiating the family guilt by opposing cigarettes.

One could wish that the others would simply wallow in guilt, if they feel so obliged, by funding hospitals or cancer research or whatever, instead of projecting their guilt upon "America" and subsidizing those out to alter or destroy the country.

The West Coast branches of Reynolds-heir money include the Tides Foundation, which interlocks with the Threshold Foundation. They have been generous to the Christics. The Southern, home-base entities are the Mary Reynolds Babcock Foundation and the Z. Smith Reynolds Foundation, both of which have donated to Christic South-bashing projects. In Washington, Smith Bagley's claim to fame is the ARCA Foundation, a most notable "deep pocket" long under the *de facto* control of Marjery Tabankin, who is a very knowledgeable radical. Her aim has been deadly, directing fire-hose volumes of Reynolds money toward a very broad array of hard-left activist groups.

Small wonder, given Tabankin's background, as provided in Poole's study of the Youth Project. She is yet another product of radical education—the University of Wisconsin, 1970. Her degree was in "the politics of urban poverty," and her postgraduate guru was Saul Alinsky of Chicago.

During the early 1970s, Tabankin was involved in activities of obvious service to the Communists, attending the Soviet-controlled World Peace Congress. She also made the pilgrimage to Hanoi, *de rigueur* for the up-and-coming radical, which brought her to the favorable attention of Jane Fonda and Tom Hayden.

After working with that pair for a while, she headed the Youth Project for several years, until the Carter Administration gave her a position of authority in VISTA—Volunteers in Service to America, supposedly the "domestic Peace Corps." Her sponsors were "Hanoi Jane" and Lee Webb, former national secretary of the radical Students for a Democratic Society (SDS). She was able to repay her California patrons by giving the Hayden-Fonda "Campaign for Economic Democracy" a fat contract to "train" VISTA volunteers in their brand of social work.

After that, Reynolds heir Smith Bagley evidently decided to let her spend his family's fortune on her pet projects, via the ARCA Foundation of Washington, D.C.

Strangely enough, it would seem that Barbra Streisand handed off control of Streisand Foundation money to Ms. Tabankin, who knows exactly what to do with everybody's money. Tabankin has recently moved West, leaving ARCA and the Streisand Foundation in other hands. She is going to mobilize the money of Hollywood women for political purposes.

Rockefeller Money

The famous Rockefeller Foundation has links to William Kunstler. In 1987, according to the records of the Foundation Center, the Rockefeller Foundation gave Mr. Kunstler his largest single donation, so that Mr. Kunstler could do what he does best.

It does not appear that any of the familiar Rockefeller organs dispensing tax-exempt funds have given directly to the Christics. However, there is the matter of consternation spreading in the wake of telephone calls to the Rockefeller Family Offices. Very likely, any "Daddy Oilbucks" money for the Christics came from there.

Marietta Davis and her superior, George Taylor, who were reached at that number, are not quite prepared to deny the matter outright—since the Christics have proudly claimed the Rockefellers as sugar-daddies—but there is a rather grim determination not to admit a thing. One is reminded, by very smooth people, that private contributions are, after all, *tres* private. All the same, small verbal slips, such as otherwise unaccountable use of the plural, lead to the suspicion that two or more members of the extensive Rockefeller clan have supported the Christics in a determinedly discreet manner. The bureaucracy which manages these family affairs also betrayed a readiness to hear about the Christics which suggests that the subject was not exactly without interest.

The name of Alida Rockefeller Messinger crops up with respect to the Threshold Foundation. Wendy Gordon Rockefeller participated in Fenton's Alar caper. Students of the Rockefeller clan could probably identify other likely suspects as well.

Rubin (Samuel P.) Foundation

This foundation has been "immortalized" in Scott Stephen Powell's great piece of investigation, *Covert Cadre*. The foundation represents "old" Communist money, and plenty of it, and has powered the Institute for Policy Studies and its very large network for decades.

It is worth noting that the Rubin Foundation split, late in 1984, one portion retaining the original name, the other becoming the Reed Foundation. The latter has not donated to the Christics, but confirmed the 1984 Rubin grant of $20,000. No later Rubin contribution to the Christics has turned up—although $2,500 was spared for the Quixote Center. It is faintly possible that money given to the "Ecumenical Ministries of Oregon" might have to do with Father Davis and the Jesuits' Oregon Province.

Lengthy lists of grants by the Rubin Foundation can serve as an interesting index of contemporary far-left projects. It is even possible that a donation by the Rubin Foundation is a "marker" indicating to satellite Marxist fund sources that the project is approved.

Vanguard Public Foundation

The "Vanguard Foundation" which the Christics say is one of their donors is probably the Vanguard Public Foundation. Whether they gave, or how much they gave, could not be ascertained. But they are a likely source. The fortune behind Vanguard belongs to Obie Benz, heir to the Wonder Bread fortune, who seems happy to have the praise of Communists ringing in his ears.

Edgar Villchur

Listed as a foundation donor by the Christics, but not listed anywhere at the Foundation Center, this benefactor was an enduring mystery. When Mr. Villchur was tracked down in Woodstock, New York, and queried about gifts to the Christics, he soared into orbit and refused to come down. How dare anyone ask that question? What business is it . . .? How did you . . .? Who told you . . .?

All spluttering aside, it seems obvious that Mr. Villchur did indeed help to bankroll the Christic vendetta. He is just outraged at having it known. It was a private matter. He is not a foundation.

Yorkin Foundation

There are two, belonging to divorced Hollywood spouses. Peg Yorkin donated, offhand, "a few thousand" to the Christics. Who can keep track of piddling sums like that?

Youth Project

Twenty years ago, the focus was on "youth." The left was doing incredibly well with the themes "turn on" to drugs, "tune in" to the propaganda line, and "drop out" of the larger society and any productive activity. But the "youths" of yesteryear, as seen at meetings and fundraisers, tend to be in the forty to seventy age range now.

Basically and characteristically, leftist groups like the Youth Project very soon eschew their commitment to deliver "services to the poor" or "the oppressed," and concentrate on trying to alter the basic institutions of the United States along lines the rest of the world is fighting to escape.

Immense sums pass into and out of the Youth Project in the sort of financial shell game one runs across in Foundation Center records. The Youth Project has given at least $55,000 to the Christics for the La Penca suit. They have been donors since Silkwood days.

Closer students of the foundation scene can see the manner in which a good deal of money-laundering could take place. Donald Jameson, a Washington-based Kremlinologist, suspects that the Rubin Foundation was making considerably larger grants than its assets could reasonably support, which could suggest the receipt of some discreet outside funds. The Funding Exchange itself, and other groups which function the same way, certainly serve to obfuscate the sources of money, and could lend themselves to laundering.

Church Money

The Christics also draw funds from Christian groups—apparently far more from Protestant denominations than from Catholic entities. Since the Christic roots are radical Jesuit roots, that seems odd, perhaps, but we must remember that "liberation theology" is Marxism camouflaged with Christian verbiage. They recognize basic "comradeship."

It is a good deal more difficult to track donations to the Christics from religious bodies or charities, because they are not under the same reporting requirements as a foundation. Information is therefore sketchy.

It seems nearly unbelievable, but the Veatch Program of the Unitarian Universalist Society, headquartered in Plandome, New York, gave a whopping $110,000 to the Christics in just two years, for the specific purpose of hounding anti-Communists in the courts and smearing them in the mass media.

It then turns out that the Veatch Program has been a reliable source of funds for *anything* the Christics do. A cozy relationship between those who control Veatch funds and Sara Nelson goes back to the late 1970s. Total donations must be enormous by now.

The Methodists and Presbyterians could hardly have done better by the

Christics. Church authorities are guarded indeed with information as to actual amounts. Suspiciously low sums, if questioned, can always be attributed to some bureaucratic cubbyhole which was "overlooked" by the public information officer.

Every now and then, word seeps out to the nice people who put money in the collection plates. Most of them would be disinclined to believe that Rob Owen, for example, is a drug-peddling murderer—and they would be right. He isn't. Therefore, they might not wish to finance those who say he is.

Yet their church hierarchy doesn't ask, but does as it pleases, passing out great gobs of church money—$11,500 here, $45,000 there—to Davis, Sheehan, and Nelson.

The Christics score very well with their invited "presentations" at various church headquarters in the National Council of Churches building in New York City. Here, they meet privately with church bureaucrats to make a professional "pitch" for funds. One could wish that, at the congregational level, skepticism prevailed, but the Sheehan snow-job videos are intended to short out clear thinking.

Tomas Borge, the Stalinist in charge of government repression in Nicaragua, can quote the Bible in what some choose to regard as a convincing manner, in support of his palpably evil program. One suspects that, if he made his pitch at the National Council of Churches headquarters, the "God-box" in New York City, he could come away a rich man!

"Peace, peace, stop the killing," is a basic message which appeals to well-intentioned people far away from the real situation. What is meant, unfortunately, is "render helpless those resisting Communism, so that the Communists can do what killing they regard as necessary in order to bring about an absence of resistance, which is called peace." At least, this has been the lesson of our century. Ignoring it is inexcusable.

But the most cursory examination of this propaganda issued by the left on the subject of Central America can leave the unwary with the notion that there is only one side. It is as if World War II were reported as a series of gratuitous acts of violence against inoffensive German, Italian, and Japanese civilians.

The author had a surprising interlude with the Rev. Leland Wilson of the Church of the Brethren. He is the lobbyist for the Church, and has offices in the Methodist Building, in Washington, D.C., where most of the Protestant church lobbyists hang their hats.

The Methodist Building, by the way, is where Flag-burner Johnson ran for sanctuary last summer. Following the Supreme Court decision, won for him by William Kunstler, with support from the Christics, Johnson called for the press to take advantage of his "photo opportunity." He proposed to burn the American flag on the steps of the Supreme Court itself.

But Congressman Bob Dornan of California and a few of the feistier aides from the nearby Cannon House Office Building came out with fire extinguishers at the ready. The message *was* clear; Johnson feared he might be spritzed, and so he ran away. He knew they would dry his tears at the Methodist Building.

Returning to Leland Wilson, he is part of Sue and Phil Wheaton's network and spoke at the anti-covert-action meeting at Johns Hopkins—the one where the Weather Underground terrorists expected to find sympathy, too. The author sought to learn how much Church of the Brethren money had been handed to the Christics, but that is Wilson's big secret.

Still, we had an opportunity to ask about Church positions, as revealed in printed handouts. What, for instance, was the religious basis for urging that South Korea be "reunited" with the regime of Kim Il-Sung? No sane Korean chooses to live under it. The cat seemed to have the Reverend's tongue.

"Are you afraid to say anything against North Korea?" we asked.

"Not afraid, no," he murmured.

Reluctant, yes. One sees adherence to the current party line, rather than either a reasoned or "moral" position. Is it the same when Wilson declaims against American covert action?

The Presbyterian Lay Committee is doing the denomination outstanding service by revealing, through their publication, *The Presbyterian Layman,* the sort of causes the collection-plate money is supporting.

Syndicated cartoonist Chuck Asay, donating his talents to the paper, depicts an all-too-familiar situation for Presbyterians anywhere outside of the church bureaucracy.

In a darkened room, someone inquires, "Is there any other business to come before the General Assembly Council."

A voice replies, "Yes, I'd like to know how much money we've sent to a Nicaraguan Marxist-Leninist group called the Antonio Valdivieso Ecumenical Center and the leftist Christic Institute?"

An outraged cry of "Who said that?" is followed by the response, "Me, Rev. Paul Scotchmer of Presbyterians for Democracy and Religious Freedom."

A great mumbling transpires—"How'd *he* get in here?" "Don't ask me, I didn't invite him," "Don't you think his question is inappropriate?" and so forth.

Finally, the Reverend Scotchmer asks, "Could we turn the lights on?"

"We'll get back to you on that, Scotchmer. Meeting adjourned!"

The vignette is "too true," as the British say. There really is a Reverend Paul Scotchmer, and he has been asking that very question, with essentially those results, for close to a year. Small wonder that the author, inquiring routinely about grants to the Christic Institute, was long stonewalled by the bureaucracy of the Presbyterian Church, USA, as it is now known. They would "get back to me," presumably in some other lifetime.

Lay Presbyterians have a problem shared with many other lay members of "mainline Protestant" churches. That is, the organizational superstructure of their church has been taken over by a coterie of leftists who regard the church as a useful item of political machinery. They have hijacked the funds, the communications system, the good name, and the basic intentions of the church. The purpose is, quite simply, use the church to bring about the "social change" the hijackers have in mind.

Secrecy and covert action are supposed to be deplorable, right? One may well ask why members of a church, any church, must be denied an accounting of church expenditures. Is there a group which has overseen the mysterious disappearance of more than five million dollars? (There is—the so-called Presbyterian Economic Development Corporation.) Then its secrets must be preserved. That is the attitude of the current overlords of the Presbyterian Church, USA, as revealed by the Lay Committee.

Laymen questioning their present "church authorities" would like to assume that they are dealing with honorable people. They tend to adopt a respectful and deferential tone, as if the old rules were still in effect. They are not, and gross deception soon becomes the fault of the victims, for being slow learners.

Slow, yes, but they are getting there anyway. The Presbyterians have recorded a loss of 1431 churches and 1,311,000 members over the period 1966–88. The overall loss of membership represents nearly 31% of the 1966 total. Worse figures are given for adult and infant baptisms, and church school membership. All the data bodes ill for the future of the denomination.

The Methodists, by the way, have suffered similarly disastrous losses of membership, as per clippings in their lobbying office. One can see why. The Elva Harper Circle is the oldest continuously-functioning women's group with the Grace United Methodist Church in Jacksonville, Illinois.

The ladies found out about the United Methodist donation of $13,500 to the Christics—in addition to $10,000 each from the World and National Divisions of the Board of Global Ministries!

Ellen Kirby—who we shall meet again in Chapter Nine—tried to smooth the feathers of the Elva Harper Circle with vague incantations about issues, problems, and questions. The ladies weren't buying it. They would make their own decisions as to how their money would be spent.

"The amount . . . given to the Christic Institute may be 'small' to you, but it represents the pledges given in good faith that it would be used to spread the Gospel of Jesus Christ—not a political agenda."

The falling-away of the disillusioned would not bother the bureaucrats, except for the sad effect it has on funds available. But they have been taking care of themselves. The July/August issue of *The Presbyterian Layman* demonstrated the clever manner in which the bureaucracy has been inflating its budgets, in order to extract more money from the dwindling membership. At the same time, in five years, they have added a million dollars to an already multi-million dollar slush fund.

They have also increased from roughly $150,000 a year to a budgeted figure of nearly $720,000 a year the amount of collection-plate money they pass along to the radicals at the National and World Council of Churches in New York.

There are, in the pages of *The Presbyterian Layman,* some encouraging clues as to the declining fortunes of the National Council of Churches itself, and its immediate neighbor, the even more presumptuous World Council of Churches. It seems there has been a drastic loss of revenues, and subsequently of staff, despite the efforts of cooperative church bureaucrats in every denomination to prevent the withdrawal of support by member congregations.

People have turned away from the "mainline" Protestant churches by the millions; some former members have simply abandoned the churches altogether, while others have chosen to affiliate with more fundamentalist and/or evangelical groups. The "mainline" church bureaucrats are probably more displeased with the latter outcome, as it is a dogma of leftist church manipulators that atheism is preferable to "the religious right."

Arie Brouwer, in a speech upon his departure from high office in the National Council of Churches, recognized aloud that "the mainline churches are becoming the sideline churches." The question becomes, do the hierarchs realize why? Twenty or more years of heedless leftist politicking have taken

116

their toll on these institutions.

And then who will support the Marxist-Leninist Antonio Valdivieso Ecumenical Center in Managua, Nicaragua, if not the rich American churches? Certainly not the Center's most cynical patron, Comandante Tomas Borge, the Sandinista Minister of Interior. The *comandantes* as a group have reduced Nicaragua to such a level of poverty that it has now displaced Haiti as the rock-bottom economic basket-case of the Western Hemisphere.

When *The Presbyterian Layman* took a harder look at "SDOP," the short-form designation for the Church's Committee on Self-Development of Peoples, it found funding of Marxist groups in Colombia back in 1972 and 1973, as well as currently in Nicaragua.

It also discovered grants from church sources to the Christics for their Sanctuary and La Penca cases. The total quoted to the author by the Presbyterian News Service was $11,170 in 1985, 1986, and 1987, with "possibly $100" since then. Keen observers of church affairs believe that figure is low.

Andy Lang is the Christics' Protestant-in-residence—at least at Arrupe House. He calls himself an "expert on the religious right." He writes criticisms of their views which find favor in the publications of the Soviet-front "Christian" group in Prague.

As editor of *Convergence,* his religious orientation is such as to run articles attacking Pat Robertson as an undesirable sort of presidential candidate. But his real work was a hatchet job on those Protestant groups fingered by Comrade Borge as uncooperative, from the Marxist-Leninist point of view.

Somehow, with Lang, the topic of mass murder arose. It is always a struggle to divert the thoughts of such people to *real* mass murder, such as the astronomical body count of Mao Zedong. If one studies the figures in the current statistical yearbooks published by the Communist government of China, one can see very easily that, just in the period 1960–62, about 56,000,000 were killed off by Mao's regime. His grand total is surely in the sixty to seventy million range.

Very odd; Lang's question was, "By starvation?" followed by a sigh of relief that it was mostly that way, yes. These people seem to think that starving to death fifty-six million people is more excusable than shooting them. The victims, although given no choice, might have different views on the subject.

Lang admitted that "within the last two years, I've had to re-think my position," on such things as Stalin's murder of, say, right around forty million people.

Of course, the only difference between now and "two years" ago is that the Moscow party line has changed. If Moscow says it is okay to notice— a generation or two late—that Stalin killed more Soviet citizens than Hitler ever dreamed of killing, then Andy Lang takes it as a green light.

And not before.

Did he, the author inquired, realize what he was revealing about himself?

"Thou Shalt Not Bear False Witness"

The Christics, with money to burn, including church money, can afford to pay their plaintiffs $50,000 a year. They have paid "key witness" Eugene Wheaton $20,000 for his services—all in small bills. Imprisoned contras in Costa Rica were offered drugs and money in exchange for testimony. Who else, in Costa Rica, was offered what?

Peter Glibbery, a British mercenary arrested in Costa Rica for serving the Contras, was seeking any way out of his dilemma and thus gave depositions to both the Avirgan-Honey team and to John Hull. His credibility suffers accordingly.

However, his statement that "the only money I have received for my subsistence was $1200 from the International Center for Development Policy," Robert White's vehicle, has not been contested. This aid was not offered to men in the same circumstances as Glibbery who did not make helpful statements.

Leslie Cockburn in her book, *Out of Control,* also reveals some of the unusual activities of Senator John Kerry's staffers, Ron Rosenblith and Jon Weiner. Senator Kerry (D-Ma.) chairs a Senate Foreign Relations subcommittee which has, in the past, shared resources with the Christic Institute, and produced reports which meshed nicely with Sheehan's views—much to the detriment of John Hull. Murky "sources" mentioned in Kerry's reports on the alleged Contra-drug connection include Glibbery.

Cockburn also notes that Glibbery was waiting for a Costa Rican presidential pardon, "for which Senator Kerry's staff had been lobbying." Bruce Jones, named as co-defendant with Hull in the La Penca suit, finds it strange that a U.S. Senator would use tax money to lobby for the pardon of a British citizen, and Jones raises the natural enough suspicion of a *quid pro quo.*

The testimony of people who will say *anything* to cop a plea, reduce a sentence, or just see a new face today, is a regular feature of the Christic line-up. A parade of hoodlums, clean-shaven and dressed in suits and ties for the television cameras, feature in pro-Christic "docudramas" which are quite intentionally deceptive to the public.

Comrade Borge and the Christians

At least it's original.

We may safely assume that no other secret-police chief in the world compares himself to St. Francis of Assisi.

We owe the following vignettes to a Maryknoll publication, *Christianity and Revolution: Tomas Borge's Theology of Life.* We asked David Mac-Michael whether Borge did not need some help from one of the (turncoat) priests in the government, in order to produce a volume on theology. MacMichael snapped, "Tomas can write his own books."

Evidently, MacMichael had not read this one, as it is not a theological treatise. It is nothing but a collection of Comrade Borge's speeches, lovingly recorded, translated, annotated, and published by the Maryknoll press. Virtually no mention is made of God, but the symbols of Christianity are brandished without mercy.

Tomas Borge is the Sandinista Minister of the Interior, in charge of prisons, police, and the enormous network of informers which Communists everywhere seem to require. He invites credulous Christian delegations visiting Nicaragua to join with him, in the spirit of St. Francis, to address "brother sun and sister moon."

How comforting it must be for such people to imagine that Comrade Borge, the old Stalinist, pauses in his work of ferreting out enemies of the state in order to harken to the birdsong.

Imagine Christians listening agog as Tomas Borge tells them that, 800 years ago, St. Francis was fighting "capitalism," even though that Marxist devil-concept was still in, shall we say, the pre-natal stage?

More than that, did you realize that "St. Francis fought Emperor Frederick Barbarossa, the Reagan of his time"? That's an unfair knock on Frederick Barbarossa. But there is a further flaw. According to the Maryknolls' own notes, St. Francis was born in 1182. Barbarossa's last invasion of Italy occurred in 1174, and Barbarossa died in 1190. So St. Francis was fighting capitalism and Reaganism at some age between eight and minus eight.

If the head of the Gestapo says a thing is true, that probably makes it true, if one lives in his country. But since the Maryknolls are headquartered in Westchester County, New York, unflattering questions arise.

One of Borge's disquisitions, "the closing address of the Sixth Continental Assembly of the World Federation of Christian Student Movements," (Managua, June 15, 1985), was entitled, "Nicaragua: Resurrected and Not to Be Crucified Again:" "Tell us, Christians, what is left for us to do? We have been crucified repeatedly . . . [Is it our duty] to go on being crucified? We have emerged from the tomb. The third day has already arrived for the Nicaraguan people," quoth Comrade Borge. This particular flight should prepare the reader for a book filled with Sandinista saints, miracles, martyrs, forgiveness of sins, and even a latter-day Sandinista "trinity".

These crudities would be offensive to real Christians—those not blinded by ideology, and/or the aura of power which Communist Ministers of the Interior tend to project.

But Andy Lang would probably love it. And, among those pictured listening to this offensive nonsense, we find the Reverend Jesse Jackson—the same Jesse Jackson who assumed Fidel Castro was a believing Christian.

The World Council of Churches has taken the money of church people and sent it to Communist Vietnam—to fund two new prison camps! The WCC, then, is paying for a Vietnamese Gulag, paying for the places of exile, horror, and despair to which people are sent for Orwellian "re-education," where they will learn to love Big Brother, or languish and die.

However, if the reader would enjoy a sample of how this notion of nice Christians in the West paying to build prisons for Communist dictators can be packaged and sold, a concise example may be drawn from one of Borge's speeches.

> A German theologian who expressed admiration for this revolution
> came to this very office and asked me how his church could help.
> We replied that we would like them to help us improve conditions
> for the prisoners. We don't like to say this publicly . . . It is not
> popular with our people, because if you were Nicaraguan . . .
> you wouldn't have much sympathy for the idea of improving
> conditions for the prisoners. When we ask Nicaraguans what they
> want us to do with the prisoners, they say "shoot them." If we
> had wanted to please our people, we would have executed them.
> That is why we asked the theologian and his associates for help
> . . . We said to them, "Don't send us resources for our children,
> who are the ones we love the most; send them for the prisoners,
> the criminals, for the murderers in the jails."

The *Los Angeles Herald Examiner's* Latin American correspondent, Merie Linda Wolin, did an extensive article on Borge in 1985, when he had been in power only six years, rather than the present ten. Some of Borge's unlovely characteristics cannot have improved with the exercise of power.

"With help from the Cubans and East Germans," Borge runs the FSLN's [Sandinista] police, state security apparatus, and prisons. Unnamed American diplomats, of the sort who would have you believe the Ortega brothers "could turn Nicaragua into a Sweden"—instead of the basket-case of the Western Hemisphere, the thing they *have* accomplished—are still willing to admit that "Borge is a dedicated Communist of the most intense type."

Borge does not conceal his love of hypocrisy; rather, he revels in it. He is famous for his two offices—one with Marxist-Leninist decor, the other emblazoned with crucifixes. Ms. Wolin describes a patently phony visit to Borge's "modest" home, where his elegantly dressed and coiffed wife went through the motions of pretending to get lunch, opening and closing empty cabinets.

The journalist Wolin knew the entire scene was fraudulent—and said so— but the charade continued, with Borge neither confirming nor denying the nature of the degrading ritual.

Borge lives at least as well as his deposed enemy, Somoza, whose standard of living seemed upper middle class, rather than luxurious. Somoza was never a hypocrite about it, never claiming he either lived like the people, or that he wished he could live in a slum, except that the security problem would not permit it. These lines are Borge's.

The reader disbelieves it? The following comments are from Borge's *Theology of Life*.

> Recently in the National Directorate we were discussing what we might do to live more closely with the poor. And the majority of the *companeros* agreed that we should live in the barrios of Managua. However . . . necessary security measures would compel us to live in a different manner . . . We couldn't, for example, go around on bicycles; for security reasons we must use motor vehicles.

So, although it broke his heart, instead of pedaling to work on his bicycle, the burden of office required Comrade Borge to move around in a BMW 733i, his personal vehicle at the time of the speech.

Wolin describes Borge as "looking like *Star Wars* Yoda without the pointed ears." He formerly claimed to have been castrated by *somocistas*, but may have dropped that particular line, now that his post-castration amatory exploits have been so extensively reported. Reed Irvine of *Accuracy in Media* has noted the number of female Western journalists who have willingly succumbed to Yoda's charms. Not that it affects their objectivity, you understand.

Nor do the female inmates of Borge's prisons get off lightly. With reporter Wolin in tow, he stroked this inmate and hugged that one. What is to prevent the women's prison from serving as a harem, when there is not a reporter present? Chivalry?

What has this to do with the Christics?

Does the elusive Father Gumshoe, "Billy" Davis, fraternize with Borge? It seems likely, although unconfirmed. MacMichael considers Borge a pal, too.

Amid the treasures to be encountered among Borge's theological musings is one that suggests a close relationship with either Davis or William Kunstler.

Far back at the beginning of this study of the Christics, looking over the selection of causes, it was possible to discern at a glance the obvious Communist interest in nearly all of them. An exception was "Big Mountain."

Here was Jesuit Father Davis and the Christic Institute, with an utterly political agenda otherwise, nobly espousing the right of a handful of Navajos to worship a landscape feature in Arizona known as Big Mountain. Christic literature avoided giving any hint of the *real* reason, but faith was present that the real reason would turn up.

It did, in one of Borge's theological flights before an assemblage of Eager Believers.

> There is nothing accidental about U.S. law number 93-531, that partitions the area known as Big Mountain . . . Peabody Coal Company, whose principal stockholder is the Bechtel Corporation—in which both Secretary of Defense Caspar Weinberger and Secretary of State George Schultz served as officers before entering government—is interested in exploiting these mineral-rich lands, without any concern for the fate of the Amerindians who were born there.

There are only two likely sources from whom Borge would have obtained the story, complete to Public Law number. One is Father Davis, the other William Kunstler. The author's wager is on Davis.

CHAPTER EIGHT

THE CHRISTICS AND
LUCKY NORTH CAROLINA

Twice, the Christics have turned their attention to North Carolina. The first time, it was to extract money for the survivors of a doctor who had given up the practice of medicine in order to become a Communist Workers' Party organizer. As a means of inspiring interest in the Party, he and other leaders had spent the better part of 1979 raiding small Klan rallies and otherwise doing their best to goad the Klan into action.

The idea was to present the Communists—who were nearly all white—as the true champions of the blacks, in hopes of recruiting a few more.

Some 75 Communists had mobbed 15 Klansmen trying to show the film *Birth of a Nation* in remote China Grove, N.C., in July of 1979. They had then traveled to Louisburg, N.C., in September to attack the Klan again. Needless to say, there was no outcry from the media or the ACLU about protecting the rights of people holding this particular brand of political opinion.

The Communist Workers' Party leaders were absolutely spoiling for a gang rumble, behaving as provocatively as possible. They had their way on November 3, 1979. A gathering of about 100 Communists, drawn by the carload from as far away as Philadelphia, assembled in a black neighborhood of Greensboro for a well-advertised "Death to the Klan" rally. The invitation had been issued; firearms were to be worn.

About 39 North Carolinians, announcing themselves to be members of the Klan and the "National Socialist Party," a splinter of the defunct American Nazi Party, accepted the invitation.

No one knows who fired first, but the Klansmen and Nazis finished it. Four Communists were killed outright, and a fifth died of wounds later. Opinion in Greensboro—a city gratuitously selected as the stage set—was that the Communists had gotten what they had asked for.

At the funeral for the victims, it was a regular Irish Republican Army scene, with earnest Communists in military field jackets doing their best to present arms—this time with better weapons.

The Trials

With four sets of videotape in existence, it was not too difficult to identify everyone present, and piece together what had happened. During 1980, those Nazis and Klansmen who were seen to have fired with deadly effect were tried for first-degree murder. But the Communists, represented by the Christics, refused to cooperate with the court, preferring to engage in street demonstrations.

While the trial was under way, the Communists gathered a few thousand comrades in Greensboro for a demonstration, vowing "death to all Klan and Nazi murderers." According to later propaganda issued from Christic headquarters, the "Greensboro Civil Rights Suit" was initiated by "survivors of the attack, represented by one of the most impressive legal teams in recent history."

Considering the behavior of the Communists, it is not surprising that, on November 17, 1980, the defendants were acquitted, the jury finding that they had fired in self-defense. Naturally, this outcome was insupportable to the left and its allies in the media. There was far more hay to be made from the event.

You see, the left loudly objects to any infiltration of violence-prone Communist groups—such as the CWP had demonstrated itself to be—but they are happy to insist upon the infiltration of their opponents. Therefore, it turns out that the Klan and Nazi groups were stiff with informers.

For instance, the Bureau of Alcohol, Tobacco, and Firearms infiltrator was trying to discover whether weapons from Fort Bragg were making their way to the Klan. The Greensboro city police informant was serving as local guide to the scene of the confrontation.

On the Communist side, the FBI had barely labeled a folder.

Nonetheless, in April of 1982, a federal grand jury indicted the Klan/Nazi men on civil rights charges. Trial resulted in a second acquittal, in September,

1982. This time, it was because the encounter was not a racial clash, despite the best efforts of the Communists to make it into one.

The Communists and their allies immediately formed the "Greensboro Civil Rights Litigation Fund," and gave Sheehan and South Carolina lawyer, Lewis Pitts, primary responsibility, despite the availability of more obviously Communist legal organizations. The list of "endorsers," however, showed that this was essentially a Communist show.

Desperate to make a "racist" issue out of what was basically a rumble among whites, Sheehan trumpeted the event as occurring in "a Black neighborhood." Yet nearly everyone was a stranger there. The bulk of the Communists had arrived in a 25-car caravan. Fifteen armed Communists had come from Philadelphia, just to bait the Klan.

There was only one black casualty in the entire fray.

The next standard tactic is to sanctify the victims. Attention was focused upon the "medical doctors" involved. The *New York Times* reverently reported that "three of the slain, and Dr. Paul Bermanzohn, who was one of those critically wounded, were trained as physicians, although at the time of their deaths, most had given up medicine for political organizing."

That was a little slip-up on the part of the *Times*. There were only two non-practicing M.D.s who sought death in the streets of Greensboro. Dr. Michael Nathan was a long-time Communist activist, previously affiliated with the Progressive Labor Party. Dr. James Waller, 37, had abandoned the healing arts to toil in a Cone Mills corduroy-finishing plant, for the sole purpose of taking over the Amalgamated Clothing and Textile Workers Union local.

Another person, evidently mistaken by the *Times* for an M.D., may have been either Harvard divinity student William Sampson, 31, who took a job "in the steamy dye room of Cone Mills White Oak plant," where he, too, was attempting to take over the local for the Communists, or Cesar Cauce, a Duke University graduate who was trying to organize "mostly Black hospital workers." (Cauce is not black.)

The Christic propaganda featured screaming headlines about "Government-Backed Right-Wing Death Squads, American Style." Sheehan and his wife Sara love this kind of hysteria.

Unfortunately, by having had informants among the Klansmen and Nazis, the Communists could claim that the affair was "government-directed," and thus "a chilling scenario reminiscent of repression in Central America"! On the same page, the Christics engage in heavy breathing because of an FBI "investigation" of the Communist Workers' Party which lasted, according to the Reds themselves, for all of ten days!

The federal civil-rights indictment, the Communists fumed, "excused the role of the Greensboro police, the [Bureau of Alcohol, Tobacco, and Firearms], the FBI, the [Justice Department] Community Relations Service, and all other agencies and officials that directed, aided, or covered up the conspiracy."

If this sounds like the Christics' shotgun approach, you are so right! There is *always* a vast conspiracy, pervasive criminality, and a "coverup." High officials are always smeared, all institutions are denigrated, and if the affair takes place in the South, it *has* to be racist, and white Southerners *must* be guilty. The only Good folks in the whole thing were the martyred Communists, who are always presented as "murdered," despite the defendants' acquittal on grounds of self-defense.

Only one of the 16 Communist plaintiffs received compensation for "wrongful death"; Greensboro paid Martha Nathan and her children $351,500. The *Times* account of 17 November 1985 went on to report that the widow of Michael Nathan "said her award would be divided among those whose spouses were killed and those who were wounded." It would be interesting to learn whether she did share it. She also "indicated that some of the money will be used to repay loans from religious organizations that backed the suit and to establish a foundation for legal aid to victims of racial violence." Since the violence was not racial, this claim merely emphasizes the disinformation aspect.

Christic South Bites Robeson County

A branch of the Christic Institute has been established in greater Chapel Hill, N.C., close to the very liberal University of North Carolina, where support is reliably forthcoming. The branch is headed by lawyer Lewis Pitts.

Of course, he is a leftist. He has headed a regional subdivision of the National Lawyers' Guild, the old left-wing standby organization of lawyers, paralegals, students—and jailhouse lawyers! Pitts was teamed with Sheehan in the Greensboro case.

Essentially, the Washington Christics have entrusted their South-bashing to the North Carolina office.

In 1988, Christic South inserted itself into a case which seemed to offer scope for shotgun-style accusations, but Lewis Pitts bit off more than he can chew.

Pitts thought he had struck gold with Robeson County, N.C. (pronounced "Robbison"). Robeson County lies between the South Carolina line and Fayetteville, and is bisected by heavily-traveled Interstate 95, the route of all sorts of snowbirds. The most common sort are elderly retirees ducking winter by heading south, but then there are others, who deal in drugs.

Aside from that, the county is an interesting piece of Americana. It contains a unique, nearly-equal mix of black, white, and Indian population. The elite now insist upon "Native American," which is not supposed to sound at all like "natives," but does. In any event, the local amalgam has developed a *modus vivendi* in which the qualities and peculiarities of each group are automatically considered, if not always appreciated.

About one marriage in eight is inter-racial, and ancient blends are common, but truth, fact, and reality are no match for the present-day mass-media propaganda. If those with access to the media say it's a racist hellhole, then that it is.

An unholy combination of the National Council of Churches, the Center for Constitutional Rights, and the Christic Institute has descended upon Robeson County and sandbagged the place. They have picked and torn at the social fabric, and cost the area between 500 and 600 new jobs, by driving off businesses prepared to locate in the county.

Mike Mangiameli, a hardbitten local newsman married to an Indian, took the trouble to check out all of the charges being made against the county, and pointed out that the crime and drug problem in Robeson County is quite average—and lower than that in the metropolitan counties whose newspapers were making the most noise.

Fourteen (not the "thirty-two" being advertised) unsolved murders are not out of line for a county of 100,000. Certainly not at a time when Our Nation's Capital, the District of Columbia, with little more than six times the population of Robeson County, is well-known as the Murder Capital of the World, racking up homicides at a rate of about 400 per year, with hardly a hope of solving hundreds of them.

Ah, but New York's William Kunstler has made a reconnaissance of the county, and smells a profitable victim. Kunstler, like the Christics, makes a lot of money by convincing rich liberals in New York and California that he is a knight-errant.

That recon was the most trivial case imaginable. Picture it—the biggest redbird in New York writing letters to an Indian school principal to tell him that he'd better let that kid wear his headband and feather in class, because the Great Spirit says he must!

When leaned upon by Kunstler, the school could only escape national infamy by saying that the boy could wear anything the Great Spirit told him to wear.

Kunstler's real interest in the matter is revealed by his statement, "there appears to be a split between older, more assimilated Native Americans, such as the principal, and younger Native Americans, like Jacobs, who are committed to regaining some of their cultural heritage."

What Kunstler and probably the majority of those who fund him want is more and deeper social divisions in America. The true "cultural heritage" of any American Indian is not what white manipulators are selling—an existence as "welfare people" excused from the real world and permitted, if not encouraged, to collapse into generations of dependency, idleness and alcoholism.

You can call that "Self-Development of Peoples," if you are a Presbyterian church bureaucrat and social meddler. You will then donate $50,000 to clever lawyers who say they can shoehorn a small faction of Robeson County citizens onto the rolls of the Bureau of Indian Affairs, with Agency numbers, and freebies that will render them an aristocracy among the local welfare people.

Hatcher and Jacobs

Although described as white on his birth certificate, one John Edward Clark had long ago decided there was no future in that. He adopted a Robeson County Indian name, Eddie Hatcher, dyed his hair black, and took to wearing beads, in the expectation of being permitted, in consequence, to indulge in less inhibited behavior. Hatcher's accomplice, Timothy Jacobs, is evidently a genuine Indian.

Having been in touch with Christic South lawyers a few days previously, Hatcher and Jacobs staged a spectacular coup on February 1, 1988. The pair barged into the offices of the county newspaper, *The Robesonian*, heavily armed and carrying chains, which they used to secure the doors. Both men had sawed-off shotguns, and Hatcher had a .38 pistol as well. The weapons were loaded, the threats were believable.

Some employees managed to escape; they spread the word that the newspaper office was being robbed, which is certainly what it looked like. Instead, it was just Eddie Hatcher grand-standing by taking hostages and threatening murder and mayhem.

Here it comes—the combined Christic-Kunstler deluge of verbiage intended to convey a terrible impression without imparting a single fact. In a half-page summary of his noble struggle on behalf of Eddie Hatcher, Kunstler's screed includes, re: drugs alone, "unsolved murders, apparently related to high-level drug dealing by county officials," "bring to justice officials believed to be holding the county hostage in (sic) a large international drug cartel," "attempting to expose the drug-trafficking attributed to highly-placed county officials."

The newspaper staff was held hostage at gunpoint from about ten in the morning until eight that night, although non-white staffers were gradually released. Hatcher placed his remaining hostages in the windows and doorways as human shields. He also announced that grenades would go off if the doors were forced. In his telephone conversation with a representative of the Governor, Hatcher sounded businesslike, while the governor's representative, Phil Kirk, came across as though he had the telephone in one hand and the hostage-situation manual in the other. (Dialogue as in official transcript.)

Kirk: As a show of good faith, would you let a few more hostages out?

Hatcher: I'm down to nine.

Kirk: You're down to nine. How about letting a few more out to show we're negotiating and talking in good faith?

Hatcher: I been lettin' 'em go all day, and I been asked the governor to call me all day, I didn't hear nothing, no hell no, I won't let one of 'em go.

The Governor's office promised Hatcher the moon, in terms of access to people other than local authorities, if he would surrender.

There was an interesting exchange with regard to acceptable jails, once Hatcher's conditions were met. Hatcher displayed his familiarity with the state's hostelries, and was quick to veto a number of them.

When offered the Orange County lockup, he first jumped at it, probably because of the magic words "Chapel Hill," but then unaccountably reconsidered.

"Ain't that a very racist county?" he inquired.

Kirk was astonished. "A racist county? No, sir, that's the most liberal county in the state."

Which explains why Carrboro was the best locale for Christic South. Here it finds supporters such as law professor Barry Nakell of the University of North Carolina.

Just as an aside, it is clear that Hatcher, or his allies, had been burning up the telephone wires to points north, because Hatcher's very next remark, after finding the Orange County jail acceptable, was to inform Kirk that he had been in touch "Mr Vernon Bellcort" (sic) of the American Indian Movement "and there's 26 [A.I.M. people] on airplanes right now on the way down here . . ."

This is interesting, because, joined with the Christic Institute in support of Kunstler's plea for the right to desecrate the flag, we find the unlikely name "Wabun-Inini Anishinabe (Vernon Bellecourt) as a representative of the American Indian Movement." It is evident that Bellecourt is part of— most likely, dependent upon—the circle which Kunstler represents, and to which the Christics also belong. Let us recall that Sheehan did his bit for the American Indian Movement's Russell Means.

Hatcher and Jacobs were brought to trial on federal hostage-taking charges in September of 1988. Christic South represented Timothy Jacobs, and William Kunstler of the Center for Constitutional Rights was to represent Hatcher with the aid of two local lawyers, Ronald Kuby and Stephanie Moore. Kunstler was busy convincing a Bronx jury of the innocence of a drug dealer accused of shooting six police officers. The North Carolina judge refused to delay the trial on that account, and told Hatcher to choose Kuby or Moore, or accept a court-appointed lawyer. Hatcher would do neither, and complained loudly of being denied his constitutional right to the lawyer of his choice.

A "racial justice group from within the National Council of the Churches of Christ" provided demonstrators for two days, to accuse the judge of bias and demand his removal from the case.

Hurling accusations at judges is yet another radical tactic. Normally this is unwise, but in media-hyped cases, especially where a racial angle can be injected, the effect seems to be to place the judge on the defensive, so that he bends over backward to demonstrate that he certainly is *not* a racist dog.

The legal question, whether or not the defendants held hostages at gunpoint and in fear of their lives for ten hours, was converted into an attack upon the county and state for racism, oppression, drug-dealing, corruption, and complicity in murder. All without a shred of evidence.

This the only tune the Christics know. It is probably the only tune they feel they ever need.

Pitts went so far as to argue that terrorizing a newspaper staff with very believable threats of death constituted the only course open to his client. (In

Kunstler's summary of this affair, the defendants merely "occupied a news-paper office to persuade the paper to print their allegations," and "sought only to compel state and local officials to address police corruption and injustice," and were thereafter cruelly persecuted.)

In keeping with the radical strategy of converting every trial into theater, not to say circus, both defendants were encouraged to tog themselves out in costumes which would look "Indian" to the media and its gullible public.

As the *Raleigh News & Observer* noted (October 2, 1988), "Almost every day last week, there has been some special request to allow into the courtroom some Indian custom, such as the single feather on a leather thong the men wear in their shoulder-length black hair. The lawyers have asked that the defendants be allowed to wear their 'medicine bags,' small leather pouches worn around the neck. Mr. Warren [another Christic lawyer] asked if Mr. Hatcher could consult with his 'spiritual advisor'."

When challenged about the sheer corniness of all this, Pitts insisted to reporters that his daily requests "are not a gimmick." Pitts said the "medicine bag" was an item that "would be like a crucifix in another culture."

Assistant U.S. Attorney Bruce produced evidence, from taped hostage-negotiation transcripts, that Hatcher had demanded to be taken into federal custody, rather than state, and that he had further demanded that the FBI not send a local agent to do so. He also wanted a federal investigation of his charges. So there were "federal demands," which are a required element under the new anti-terrorism statute.

But Jacobs was acquitted because he had not personally made the demand, and Hatcher, perhaps because the "demand" seemed rather trivial, as demands go. The acquittal caused the usual remarks on the unpredictable nature of juries.

From New York, Kunstler, who had never shown his face in the courtroom, "compared both men's actions to the Boston Tea Party," according to news accounts.

Leftist pressure then focused on preventing an indictment on state kid-napping charges. Pitts claimed that would constitute double jeopardy.

We may recall that the Nazi and Klan members endured what might be considered triple jeopardy, and there was a smug satisfaction about that. Whenever the left doesn't like the outcome of a state trial, it tries for a federal trial in hopes of a more satisfying verdict.

Followed, if possible, by a Danny Sheehan civil suit!

At any rate, Hatcher and Jacobs found themselves indicted on state charges on December 7, 1988. Jacobs had already left the state, but Hatcher was slower off the mark. He was jailed. Bail was initially set at $140,000, in view of the likelihood that he would skip the state, as he had done prior to his federal trial.

Bail was eventually reduced to $25,000, something the National Council of Churches felt able to forfeit. Hatcher did run away, and the N.C.C. did forfeit the bond—something one assumes was not communicated to church members whose money it was.

Both men turned up at the Onondaga Reservation in upstate New York, possibly on Kunstler's advice. There they might have remained indefinitely, in theory, but neither of them could stand the place. Jacobs took to speeding over the countryside, and was finally bagged by state troopers after he crashed into the rear of a school bus in Madison County.

The noisy left invited New York's Governor Mario Cuomo to delay extradition until the New York Attorney General could pass upon the quality of justice in North Carolina. True, the governor of that state was a Republican, and to the possible scoring of partisan points, Cuomo might add the admittedly evanescent gratitude of New York's considerable population of actual Communists and the insufferable radical-chic groups of Manhattan.

On the other hand, if Cuomo entertained the faintest notion of taking the South in some future run for the presidency, then inserting himself into this noisy but trivial case in a major Southern state might prove unwise, in the longer run.

Meanwhile North Carolina had found nothing but "rumors and gossip" in the wild accusations. But that never prevents the Christics from re-packaging and recycling the same old merchandise—or the press from broadcasting it again. Christic South now called it a *civil* suit, charging the governor, the attorney general, the head of the state bureau of investigation, and assorted other officials with their standard blather.

Now, the purpose of the civil suit became painfully transparent when an affidavit from Neal Rose, District Attorney in Madison County, New York, made it clear that the suit was intended as a plea-bargain ploy. Neal was engaged in discussions pertaining to the extradition of Timothy Jacobs, "during which time Mr. Pitts stated that the civil lawsuit which had been commenced in the Federal Court of the State of North Carolina could and would be summarily dropped if a satisfactory plea bargain of the charges pending in Robeson County, North Carolina, could be obtained."

Further, the District Attorney concluded, "the clear implication of Mr.

Pitts' remarks was that there was no factual basis for the lawsuit . . ."

Madison County Judge William O'Brien, complaining of the carnival atmosphere, ordered the extradition. Possibly Jacobs had heard a court officer in Madison County remarking that the rapist who had represented himself before the judge, in the previous case heard, "had a better lawyer than Jacobs." At any rate, Jacobs accepted court-appointed counsel and pleaded guilty to state kidnapping charges on May 5, 1989; he was sentenced to six years. The general tenor of opinion was that Jacobs had been taken for a ride by Hatcher and his radical friends, and that he deserved some jail time, but not a whole lot.

Hatcher, for his part, scooted around the United States in the magical manner that says someone else is picking up the travel tab. He presented himself at various Indian reservations in the West, possibly in what he fancied to be Indian costume, but could not seem to convince genuine Indians of what the press, the church radicals, and the activist lawyers wanted everyone else to swallow.

He made it as far as California, where his final move was to seek asylum at the Soviet Consulate in San Francisco. The Soviets, rightly figuring that violent troublemakers of his sort ought to remain in the United States, for best effect, turned him over to the FBI. Hatcher was eventually hauled back to North Carolina, and held for trial.

Meanwhile, according to some, film and book offers have been arriving. However, dreams of riches are dimmed by a judge's warning that any money derived from such sources must be placed in a fund to compensate victims of the kidnapping. Of course, that would only apply to money earmarked for Hatcher and Jacobs. If the actual perpetrators were cut out of it, the propaganda extravaganza which the Communists are always capable of mounting could produce bags of money for "movement" people.

Christic South, no longer needing a plea-bargain tool, and having milked its sensational accusations for maximum contributions and media impact, decided to try, very quietly, to drop the civil suit. Not so fast, was the response. Pitts and his cohorts had sullied the reputations of top officials. "Such allegations . . . carry an enormously stigmatizing effect that lingers long beyond the plaintiffs' voluntary dismissal of this action."

But that *is* the Christic brand of legal terrorism.

The North Carolina Attorney General's office filed a motion in U.S. District Court, asking for Rule 11 sanctions against Pitts, Kunstler, and Barry Nakell, a University of North Carolina law professor who was pleased to participate in this affair, when it seemed to offer leftist glory.

These sanctions were imposed in September 1989. Christic South's lawyers, Pitts and Nakell, as well as William Kuntsler, may not practice law in the Eastern District of North Carolina until heavy compensation to the state has been paid.

Rule 11 exists for the purpose of disciplining lawyers who introduce frivolous and/or groundless lawsuits. "The signature of an attorney or party constitutes a certificate by him that he has read the pleading, motion, or other paper; that to the best of his knowledge, information, and belief formed after reasonable inquiry it is well-grounded in fact and is warranted by existing law or a good faith argument . . . and that it is not interposed for any improper purpose, such as to harass or cause unnecessary delay or needless increase in the cost of litigation . . ."

Lawyers for the State of North Carolina required thirty pages to detail the sins of omission and commission on the part of the Christic law team and William Kunstler. In conclusion, they state:

> As officers of this Court, Mr. Pitts, Mr. Nakell, and Mr. Kunstler filed two complaints without proper foundation in either law or fact and, according to Mr. Pitts' own statements, for the purpose of influencing a plea bargain in a pending state criminal action. Such misconduct offends every prong of Rule 11. Such misconduct holds to public ridicule and scorn high state officials, including fellow officers of this Court, when no evidence suggests even one of those officials ever violated his professional responsibility or his public trust. Plaintiffs' counsels' misconduct utilizes the power and dignity of this Court as a propaganda and plea bargaining tool for persons rightfully charged with serious criminal offenses under the North Carolina criminal laws . . .

There is more to the misbehavior of Christic South's lawyers. For example, Pitts persists in finding sly ways of practicing law in the state without being a member of its bar. He was also cited for contempt during a bench conference, and sentenced to three hours of jail time, although the judge failed to follow through on this. His offense was the now-standard Christic one of accusing the judge of being in league with the defendants.

Predictably, Pitts is attempting to wrap this matter in the skirts of the Constitution. This is all a conspiracy to chill, to silence, to seek revenge against these selfless paladins of justice. In fact, Pitts cries darkly to potential supporters, it is part of the "larger national attack on the Christic Institute."

This, of course, refers to the Rule 11 penalties laid against the Christics by the federal court in Miami.

This cry of "they're all against us," would be derided as right-wing paranoia, had it emanated from a right-wing source. But it will be heard repeatedly, for as long as the Christics are permitted to stay in business.

CHAPTER NINE

CHRISTIC "BAD BEHAVIOR"

Jailed by Docudrama

Sheehan's September, 1987 boast that he intended to deprive his defendants "of everything they have" and see that they "get put in jail for the rest of their lives" almost worked out, in the case of John Hull, in early 1989.

Basically, the Christics took their case, after it was thrown out of court in Miami, to San Jose, Costa Rica. With President Arias' confidant, John Biehl, having the influence he does, the left felt assured of a better reception.

It seems incredible, but John Hull was arrested, on January 12, 1989, on the "evidence" of Leslie Cockburn's "West 57th Street" docudrama, based, like her book, on Avirgan, Honey, and Sheehan's assertions. This 68-year-old man was thrown into prison, without bail, without his needed medication, and then long denied treatment, when he suffered a heart attack.

He received mail from Methodists of his home-town congregation, people who knew him, and therefore did not believe for one moment that he was a drug trafficker, and who could probably figure out, more or less, where the accusations were coming from.

Having time for a lengthy response, Hull composed by candlelight in his cell—"a three-candle letter," he called it—a message to the folks back home in Indiana. It was dated February 24, 1989.

While expressing gratitude for the outpouring of mail, he remarked, "The irony of some of the messages helped to bring a smile. The card from Jim and Jeanne Bishop starts, 'Streaming through your window may the sunshine send its rays . . .' "

"I am being held in solitary confinement in a cell 6' by 10'. It has a window about six inches square with a steel plate welded two inches outside so that air can get in but no sunshine."

What the Costa Rican authorities wanted was made plain to him in the beginning. All he had to do was to sign a statement that "the communist propaganda, put out on national TV by the CBS 'West 57th Street' program, was true. I could walk out a free man with no publicity."

"I was told that, if I refused, I would be in prison for 12 months without bail before a trial, and I probably wouldn't live the year . . ."

Music to Danny Sheehan's ears!

After an initial softening-up period "in a cold cell in undershorts for 24 hours," he was moved to a $10' \times 12'$ cell "with eight bunks and 26 inmates. There was no water and no bathroom in the cell, and the door was closed from 7:00 PM until 6:30 AM, which meant we had to urinate and defecate on the floor. The men tried to sleep two or three to the bunk with the others on the floor."

He was then moved to a section of the prison with 80 beds and 149 inmates. "Sixty-nine men had to go free before I even had a concrete bunk."

There were ten cells with eight bunks apiece, and 13 or 14 men in each.

"The first thing the inmates told me in my cell was that there was a contract out to murder me in prison. The cell leader then smiled and put his arm around me and said, 'That is the bad news. The good news is that it will not happen here.' "

Hull is a respected man in Costa Rica, and the respect extended to inmate level, even if not all the way down to venal politician level.

"We have decided that we will accompany you at all times. That means to the bathroom, to the chow line, wherever you go. Also, we will put a bench in front of the cell entrance, and one inmate will be there at night."

Hull was in for even more astonishing news. "Whether you want to admit it or not, you are old and you are sick, while I am young and healthy," the cell leader told him. He thereupon gave up his bunk to him!

As Hull wrote to the members of his congregation at home, "That night, as I lay in the darkness in his bed, I did some serious soul-searching. Would I have the faith, the kindness, and the courage to give up my bed and be lying there on a hard cold concrete floor to act as a decoy for an assassin? Would I do these things for a person I did not know? Would I even do it for someone I did know?"

He left them with this thought, for "when the sermon gets dull." He suggested, "Count the number of people there that would do what this dark-skinned young Catholic was doing for your Methodist friend John Hull."

However, Hull's troubles had only begun. He suffered a heart attack on a Saturday morning, and was permitted no medical assistance, even though his own doctor came to the prison; he could only talk to him, not even examine him. The following Monday evening, he was taken to a well-equipped San Jose hospital, but the doctor didn't like the idea of treating a man chained to a wheelchair, so he was shunted along to another hospital.

"They wanted to start IV tubes, run an electrocardiogram, and get me on a heart monitor. They could not do any of these things until the handcuffs were removed." The protests of higher and higher authorities at the hospital meant nothing; the guards had their orders—Hull stayed shackled to the gurney. Finally the chief surgeon introduced himself to Hull and said, "I don't know you, but I know of you, and I am ashamed of my country."

Eventually, the doctors were allowed to do their work. But there was to be a constant contest between the doctors and nurses trying to keep him alive and help him recover, and those who would rather he did not.

There is much more to the two-month ordeal. About three weeks after the date of the letter from which we have quoted, Hull was allowed out on huge bail. He remained on his farm while the media-generated clamor continued; Avirgan and Honey were in their element!

"They are going to lose everything they have," Sheehan tells his faithful. Hull was stripped of assets and had no money for his own defense, and naturally, he was concerned about his precarious health—not improved by jail time—and the threats to his life, in and out of jail, in Costa Rica itself.

Rather than feature in another "West 57th Street" docudrama, he departed for the United States in late July—without the permission of Senores Arias and Biehl. Here, he was hospitalized for another ten days, and then returned to Indiana to recuperate.

Hull's long letter included the following remark, which might well be addressed to all the bureaucrats and hierarchs of the "mainline churches" who have donated to the Christics:

> It is not my intention to judge the Methodists or any other church. However, you have no idea how deep the hurt is, knowing the Methodist hierarchy is a generous supporter of the left . . .

Hull had been describing, not his own situation, which he did not then know was being fueled by a minimum of $36,000 from Methodist collection-plates, but the situation of the contras and their families, brutalized and driven from their homes by the Sandinistas.

Courtroom Antics

The Christic Institute now carries the dubious distinction indeed of being the only entity ever sanctioned *twice* under Rule 11 of the Federal Code of Civil Procedure. This rule, rarely applied, is a last ditch defense of the judicial system itself against abuse by those filing frivolous, groundless, or harassing lawsuits.

For instituting the La Penca lawsuit without having—or being able to develop—any credible evidence, Judge James Lawrence King of Miami sanctioned the Christics in February of 1989. In September of that same year, Judge Malcolm J. Howard of the Eastern District of North Carolina came down on Christic South, as we have seen.

Defense lawyers have amassed a compendium of additional examples of misbehavior on the part of the Christic legal terrorists.

First and foremost, the Christics have used their superior access to the mass media to "try" the case by propaganda barrage. Defense lawyers also note "defamatory and perjurious" statements which have gushed forth in a steady stream since the suit was first announced.

As an example, they cite the "American Excess Cheque," which the Christics spread around the courtroom and around the country. It states, "During the Viet Nam War Richard Secord, John Singlaub and others in the CIA imported heroin from S.E. Asia into the United States. Today these same people are importing cocaine from South America. They have used this drug money to assassinate political opponents, overthrow governments, and enrich themselves. They have become a government unto themselves."

This totally false and appalling screed may, indeed, be the product of a lawyer, but certainly not of a responsible or ethical lawyer. This is the product of a rabble-rouser who is untroubled by the utterance of truly vicious lies.

The canons of ethics require that an attorney refrain from "extrajudicial statements" likely to prejudice the outcome of a case. The La Penca case was designed and intended, from the beginning, to be a media event, and the Christics' every word has been generated in hopes of prejudicing the outcome of the case in their favor.

"Plaintiffs' attorneys have appeared on every major network proclaiming that Defendant Singlaub, among others, has been [named as] a drug-smuggler, a murderer, an assassin, and/or traitor." The Christics' assertions are totally false, but the Big Lie works well for anyone plugged in to the mass media.

The interesting business of a lawyer paying his clients, rather than the other way around, is also unethical. Mostly, lawyers do not pay their clients because it's no way to run a business, and *pro bono* work is the limit of their generosity.

But, with the trio of Sheehan, Nelson, and Davis, the desire to bring this lawsuit was so strong that they paid witnesses and paid plaintiffs. Avirgan and Honey were, at first, paid $1,600 a month, according to Martha Honey's deposition. Tax returns for the Christics later reveal a flat $50,000 a year paid to the plaintiffs.

The defense also points to the sheer quantity of hearsay, the enormous mass of inadmissible nonsense which appears in the "Sheehan affidavit." Surely it calls into question Sheehan's legal education, ethical standards, or both. A prime example is found in the thousand pages of paid, rambling hearsay by Gene Wheaton, who is Source 24 as well as 48. Sheehan was perfectly well aware that Wheaton had no first-hand knowledge of General Singlaub's activities or those of Ted Shackley, yet used him as not one, but *two* secret sources.

Small wonder that Sheehan was concealing his witnesses. An attorney stakes his reputation on statements in which he swears, as an officer of the court, that he has solid grounds for believing these things to be true. Yet no one knew better than Sheehan that his witnesses did *not* have the knowledge or information attributed to them.

Sheehan obstructed the work of defense attorneys for nearly a year, by refusing to identify, much less produce, his 79 witnesses. When Judge King threatened to throw the case out of court if he did not do so, the secret finally tumbled out. The sorry picture of unidentifiable, non-existent, duplicated, and disavowing witnesses grew by the day.

The case was turning upon the double hearsay of Gene Wheaton and the triple and sometimes quadruple hearsay of no-surname David in Costa Rica— the kidnapped-tortured-murdered-buried David who is walking around and saying he never heard of the people Sheehan has linked to him by concocted testimony.

As for disruptive courtroom behavior, the Christics have a tradition by now of trying to punch out judges before they get any ideas about not seeing things Danny's way. The Christics let them know about their superior access to the media, and their uninhibited use thereof. Judges soon learn that they might become the "heavy" in a docudrama or a full-fledged movie.

In the Silkwood affair, even though Sheehan never reached first base in an actual courtroom, he managed to induce not one, but *two* federal judges to excuse themselves from the case.

With the La Penca case, Sheehan let Judge King know that the glop-guns were loaded and aimed. What Sheehan "had" on Judge King is that he was a Nixon appointee, he didn't rack Bebe Rebozo, and some bad people have been known to use the bank with which he is affiliated. It has been said that Christic "investigators" have surveilled the judge.

Sheehan does not fail to inform his financial supporters that Judge King is a bad person. Ellen Kirby, of the Methodist Church Women's Division, told the author darkly that she "ought to look into that judge down there." This was in response to a hint that all was not right with the lawsuit, and that the churches may find that they had been paying people to bear false witness.

Whether this initial challenge, the public accusation of bias and criminal association, caused Judge James Lawrence King to extend an uncommon degree of patience to Sheehan and the Christics is not known. Nevertheless, it seems to many that uncommon patience was indeed extended.

During the interminable hearings on the La Penca case, Sheehan wanted "discovery, forever"; he wanted the court to give him permission to delve back to 1959 in the lives and records of the defendants, in hopes of filling in his "pattern of racketeering" which he claimed existed.

The judge was trying to focus Sheehan's mind on the job he had elected to take on—that of proving a connection between the bombing at La Penca and *any* of his defendants.

But Sheehan did not like being thwarted in his attempt to prowl endlessly through the papers and effects of his chosen victims, in hopes of producing his revisionist history of the world in our time, or whatever other purpose he and his circle of acquaintances may have had.

Judge King entertained some hope of getting this show on the road, after two years, yet Sheehan whined, "Does the court have a fetish with insisting that a case go to trial within a confined period of time . . .?"

Judge King retorted, "I think you are bordering on disrespect . . . I do have a sincere belief that every lawsuit that is filed in any federal court can and should be tried, in the interests of the litigants, within a three-year period of time at the outside."

It was in the interests of the Christics to drag out proceedings as long as possible. Their "evidence" was in sad shape, but the case was doing a great job of fund-raising. It provided endless opportunities for character assassination, and of course it kept the defendants pinned down and drained of resources.

A court record is rarely amusing, but watching Sheehan play wheedle, needle, and quibble with the judge, while the judge tries to stay sane, is an episode which comes close.

Upon hearing that summary judgment had been awarded to the defendants, in June of 1988, attorney Sheehan threw a tantrum and announced that the judge had "joined the secret team." That is, Sheehan was accusing Judge King of becoming *part* of his purportedly vast, nefarious, enduring racketeering conspiracy.

The tantrum continued, with Sheehan calling the ruling "transparently foolish . . . extraordinary and bizarre," and accusing the judge of trying to save Presidential candidate George Bush from the devastation Sheehan was about to wreak upon him.

When Rule 11 penalties were assessed against Avirgan and Honey, as well as the Christic Institute and Daniel Sheehan personally, Sheehan announced in a huff that there was "no way" the penalties would be paid.

"Judge King's decision is a legal disgrace," Sheehan stormed, "It's absolutely preposterous to think anybody's going to ever pay this money." (Cooler heads prevailed; the money to save Sheehan's Institute was gathered from leftists who loved the story, and would never surrender the dream of ruining good men.)

Daniel Sheehan was desperately anxious to insert himself into the special prosecutor's act, in the Iran-Contra case, thrusting selections of his "discovery" plunder to Lawrence Walsh, whether he wanted the material or not.

When a dispute developed, during the North trial, over the secrecy of certain documents, Sheehan virtually ran into the street, displaying the papers to the press. He had extracted them from Robert Owen, while in the process of grabbing everything which might possibly aid in proving his own case.

Judge Gerhard Gesell had to use icily sharp language on Sheehan, when he tried in other ways to interfere in the North case. On January 9, 1989, Gesell reported that the Christic Institute wanted him to postpone a ruling, although the Institute lawyers had zero standing before the court in this case.

But Sheehan is not the man to take a hint. Two weeks later, Judge Gesell issued another reproach, saying "This Institute has been attempting, by telephone calls to the Court's chambers, to influence the Court's action on pending motions. I believe that type of effort, for which I hold counsel [Sheehan] responsible, is so clearly improper that any responsible lawyer would have prohibited it.''

Nevertheless, Christic propaganda was found ''on tables in the courtroom'' when it opened for business. Judge Gesell had it removed, and complained, ''There are boxes [of this material] piled up in my chamber. I don't need that.'' The judge added, ''I have not read any of the material.''

Lewis Pitts has adopted most, possibly all of Daniel Sheehan's tactics. During the Robeson County case, Pitts used a great deal of body language to convey disgust, exasperation, feigned incredulity and so forth, to send messages to the jury which would not be tolerated verbally. Getting away with that, Pitts responded to some adverse ruling by suggesting noisily that the judge ''might as well pull up a chair'' at the prosecutor's table. On the second occasion, Pitts was reportedly cited for contempt—but, alas, the judge forget to impose any sanction.

When Pitts went to upstate New York to try to prevent the extradition of Timothy Jacobs, he managed to infuriate a Madison County judge with his antics. An extradition hearing is a rather cut-and-dried affair, legally; there are only a few clear-cut points to be established. The judge did not appreciate the circus atmosphere, the media-grabbing theatrics, which are part and parcel of the Christic ''act,'' and was more than happy to send Pitts and his client back South.

The second rule 11 penalty may have the much-needed effect of telling the world—the legal world, and possibly the foundation world or the National Council of Churches world—that the Christics are bad-news incompetents.

As an amusing note, Christic South has even visited trouble upon William Kunstler. Kunstler told the court that he had relied upon University of North Carolina law professor Barry Nakell, and thus ''had no personal knowledge of the facts justifying the complaint.'' The judge reminded Kunstler that this was, in itself, ''a violation of Rule 11.''

The whole mess brought Kunstler a personal $10,000 sanction, and a share of the $92,834.28 liability laid against Pitts and Nakell as well. And none of these three may practice law in the Eastern District until it is paid. Kunstler may not find that inconvenient, but Christic South certainly will.

Kunstler can ask his patrons at the Rockefeller Foundation for the extra money. Perhaps the Reynolds clan will bail out Christic South. But one could hope that these benefactors would think harder about what they are doing.

Professor Nakell's explanation to his students of Judge Howard's comments upon his own competence should provide a degree of campus merriment.

Phone Harassment

The law firm engaged to defend General John Singlaub, and which did by far most of the work on the case, is Spencer and Klein, in Miami.

Aside from one or two of the more prominent defendants, the defense lawyers in Miami took the heaviest harassment "hits." Poison-pen letters are a bit old-fashioned, now that poison-phone calls are available instead. Not that receptionists at Spencer and Klein ever grew accustomed to having scorpions drop out of the poison-pen mail.

During the Vietnam War, American fifth-columnists used poison-phone calls to add to the distress of the families of prisoners of war. The practice is hardly new. Some of the technique, however, turns out to be quite advanced. For a period of several months immediately prior to the judge's decision to award summary judgment to the defense in the La Penca civil suit, Spencer and Klein endured what must be called an unprecedented assault by phone.

The earliest victim was an elderly secretary who quit rather than endure the anonymous threatening phone calls directed at herself and her husband personally. Then there was Rosie Gonzalez, who handled public relations. She was able to shrug off the standard death threats, but was unnerved when a caller announced that he had kidnapped her son—and described what he was wearing that day—and that he would kill him unless the law firm stopped defending Singlaub. She quit her job, too.

Thomas Spencer, lead lawyer for the defense, received death threats at the office and at home. But perhaps even the anonymous callers were becoming bored with the same old thing. As a result, one day, when Spencer was in Washington for a deposition, his son received a call from someone purporting to be at the hospital with his father, and said he had been shot and critically wounded.

There was strong suspicion that headquarters for Harassment Central was in a building which could observe the law firm's office suite, but investigators never seemed able to pinpoint the apartment. Callers could track people as they moved through the offices. More astonishingly, they could cause any phone to ring without having the call go through the switchboard, cause all the phones to ring at once, and/or continually, and they could—and did—tap into calls, cutting them off, listening in, or interrupting conversations.

General Singlaub was called at Spencer's office to be informed that sniper rifle crosshairs were on him.

This treatment was openly linked to the Christic Institute case. While the Christics would undoubtedly deny any connection with it and find it ritually deplorable, these are their allies. But the suspicion lingers that a touch of extra-legal harassment would not be an unwelcome addition to the Christic arsenal.

CHAPTER TEN

WHY DO THE CHRISTICS DO IT?

Do the Soviets have an interest in trying to punish or destroy leading anti-Communists in the United States?

Do the Soviets have a interest in stopping American, not Communist, covert action? Causing us to abandon another army in the field—the contras? Having us grow accustomed to impotence and defeat, when confronted by Communist dictators, however weak? Having us accept a powerful fifth (or first) column within the United States? Weakening first the Reagan, then the Bush administrations?

In every case, obviously.

Does the Christic lawsuit advance all of these Soviet interests?

Obviously.

Was the La Penca lawsuit initiated in order to advance Soviet interests?

Here we enter difficult ground.

There is no present defector from the Politburo of the Communist Party of the Soviet Union, or the KGB, who can state, in an American court of law, "Yes, I know these people. We worked together on the plan. I directed them. They were rewarded thusly."

On the other hand, we have here a group of Americans who openly admit to working with the Communists. Why not? they ask. All our friends do, too. "The churches do it." Very true.

Are the Christics, then, professionals or enthusiasts?

Or is there a continuum? There is a "feel," here, of enthusiasts gliding over into professionalism.

Idealism as a Motive

First, let us dispose of this possibility. A full-fledged Jesuit has no trouble sounding high-minded, nor has a lawyer. Davis and Sheehan seem to have their own mystical "Christic" frills, if Gerry Spence is to be believed. Davis was glad to take credit for influencing God to have a tornado touch down in the very same county as the Kerr-McGee plant, at the very time it was needed to make a point to the jury, according to Spence!

This sort of thing does not appear in the Christics' videotaped *spiel* on "the secret team," however. It might offend, or cause unseemly mirth among, their large contingent of followers who are far from religious.

So, now, we find these high-minded people banded together to fight the forces of evil, and we have met those chosen as worthy targets. Are they mass murderers? Fond of round numbers, the Christics like to pin 40,000 deaths on Shackley, and attribute 100,000 to Singlaub.

No particular evidence is adduced, except that these men were in positions of authority during the war in Southeast Asia, more or less when the Communists say this many supporters of theirs were killed. How do we know they were supporters? Simple. Red hearts don't bleed for just anyone.

But, let's talk mass murder. We have the Red Khmer (Khmer Rouge) genocide in Cambodia, when mere literacy was a death sentence. Even wearing glasses was a death sentence; that was the Khmer Rouge rough-and-ready definition of an intellectual.

According to the Sheehan affidavit and the equally authoritative Christic Comix, the defendants are world-class bloodthirsty criminals fighting against "reformist governments." The death toll exacted by those Cambodian reformers amounted to a larger proportion of the available population than any other round of social reform in this century so full of social reform.

The roll call of Communist atrocities in this century is unprecedented. The various Communist parties of the world have brought premature death to more people than any other gang in the history of the human race. And the real carnage begins after resistance has ended!

Think about it. Let it sink in. This is literally and incontrovertibly true. We are talking about more than one hundred million dead, all within the lifetime of our older citizens.

But, during many months of extensive reading of Christic literature and viewing of Christic videotapes, the author has encountered no word which even acknowledges this prime fact of the Twentieth Century. No leading light of the Christics has provided a hint of condemnation of this historically unprecedented slaughter.

So much for idealism. It's a non-starter as a motive.

Other Possible Motives

The Christics evidence an enthusiastic hatred for the leading defendants; the author detects nothing faked about that. Is it something personal, a matter of ideology, massive self-deception, or a coldly professional fingering of targets?

How about "all of the above?"

Theodore Shackley, while trying to fathom what he was doing in this lawsuit, had a chat with Father Davis. "Chief investigator" Davis was totally disinterested in anything Shackley had to say. Shackley might be pure as the driven snow re: La Penca, but according to Davis, he was still going to receive the full Christic treatment.

Suppose, however, that Davis believed that the CIA, with Shackley as its devil-figure, had brought down the Communist government of Salvador Allende. With Davis, it would be an article of faith—and we do not say that lightly—that Allende was Good and those who deposed him were Evil. Davis might then have an embedded personal, political, and even "religious" hostility, quite impervious to reason.

Also in this picture is John Biehl, former advisor to Allende, current advisor to Costa Rican President Oscar Arias. We have the Office of the President of Costa Rica sharing with the Christics the expense of publishing the latest version of Avirgan and Honey's charges. Does Biehl hold a personal and political grudge against anti-Communists? Obviously. Only John Hull was within reach, so John Hull was to be smeared, plundered, imprisoned—and if he died of it, great.

As for self-deception, with the "activist children of the Sixties," there is a permanent spoiled-brattiness which insists upon having its way, and throwing tantrums until indulged. In the case of both Sheehan and Nelson, converting their opinions into public myth or popular fact has become a profitable and personally very satisfying line of work.

Sheehan might well be convinced of the story he has created. As for Nelson, one can imagine a total indifference to whether her husband's yarn bears any resemblance to reality, so long as it loosens the purse-strings of all those folks on the donor-list.

An analogous question might be, does Jackson Browne, a pop singer, believe the words to his song? Is he sincere, or is it a good act? Does his agent or business manager believe the words? Finally, does their belief or disbelief have any bearing whatsoever on the truthfulness of the message?

Surrogate Service

We have looked at the "major defendants," men who have devoted their lives to fighting our wars and resisting Communist imperialism. At the same time, we have seen that their assailants have devoted themselves to weakening the United States and supporting our enemies.

Do they actually work for the Communists? Well, David Fenton does. As a registered foreign agent for Communist governments, as well as for Communist guerrillas attacking recognized governments, he is paid directly for his services. That his client list has included the Christic Institute tells us something unpleasantly revealing about the Institute.

How about the plaintiffs, Avirgan and Honey? *De facto* traitors during the Vietnam War, probable informers for Marxist dictators, propagandists for leftist forces and regimes anywhere, and suspected by the U.S. Ambassador and CIA chief of station in Costa Rica of being Sandinista agents—quite a record.

Avirgan and Honey willingly, enthusiastically, fed into enemy intelligence during the Vietnam War. Why should they do any less now? There has been no change of heart. Nor have there been any penalties.

All of the causes espoused by the Christic trio, and they are superficially quite varied, are in harmony with the Communist line. The anti-nuclear campaign, the "sanctuary movement," South-bashing, stirring racial animosities, defending criminals or terrorists whose motives are loudly leftist— these have been previous Sheehan and Nelson causes.

Is Father Davis in solidarity with the Communist and radical Jesuits of Latin America? It seems quite likely. He has publicly expressed his solidarity with the Communist Party and Fidel Castro. Like his associates, he defends the Sandinistas by "investigating" Americans who oppose them. He has aligned himself with the faction of the priesthood which trashed Pope John Paul II during his visit to Managua.

The Vatican, which does not lightly declare Jesuit priests *suspensus a divinis* (suspended from priestly duties) apparently found good reason to suspend Father Davis about five years ago. All the available data suggests he remains suspended, forbidden to offer the sacraments or to say mass, forbidden to preach.

The most open service which Daniel Sheehan has performed for the

Communists was in the Greensboro case. He is quick to flash the words "Nazi" and "Klan," but his lawsuit was really against the City of Greensboro, North Carolina. It was Greensboro which had to pay off the widow of the Communist Party member who came to North Carolina for the purpose of engaging in a gun-battle in the streets of the city.

Now we may remind ourselves of a curious matter cited earlier. The Christics, in their plea for ever-broader power to subpoena the papers of the major defendants, referred to check stubs in Singlaub's records which "indicate he also has a program to aid the 'freedom fighters' of Afghanistan." Typically, the Christics characterized this as a "continuing . . . criminal racketeering activity."

When the father of Charles Horman was induced to file suit against American officials, blaming them for the death of his son in Chile, intelligence experts believe that Peter Weiss and William Kunstler had but one purpose. They hoped to force information from the U.S. government about political affairs which were of major importance to the Communists.

Precisely the same objective may have animated Sheehan's attempt to follow up on clues, found in Singlaub's check stubs, about the support of Afghan resistance forces fighting the Soviet Army in Afghanistan.

Not even Sheehan can *really* believe that supporting resistance to foreign invasion is a criminal racketeering conspiracy. So why did he clamor for more information on the Afghan resistance? One very good reason would be to extract intelligence material for the benefit of the Soviet invaders.

Does anyone have a more plausible theory?

Christic supporters in the entertainment world include, according to Father Davis, "Hanoi Jane" Fonda and Ed Asner, two of the most open supporters of communist regimes in Hollywood. And then we have Kris Kristofferson, who says he believes that America deserves to be occupied by the Soviet Union.

And only the Communists sent a reporter to the Christic fund-raiser in January, 1989. The Christics are part of *their* world.

The Soviet-controlled World Peace Council glorifies the Christics. Davis is the subject of friendly interviews in the Communist *People's Daily World*. Cliff Kincaid, then with *Accuracy in Media*, revealed this and more during a TV debate with Sheehan on November 25, 1987. The Christics' Andy Lang writes for the Soviet-front Christian Peace Conference, and has attended its meetings in Prague.

Former Christic David MacMichael served to link the Christics with the

Philip Agee and Louis Wolf turncoats. Not that there has been any loss of contact since his departure. It is interesting to note that the Christics have entered into some sort of alliance with *Geheim,* a West German far-left propaganda and support group which shares many Christic goals, spreads Christic propaganda in German, and may assist in West European fund-raising.

If—or when—the Communist governments of Nicaragua, Cuba, or the Soviet Union are offered the services of Americans desperately keen to help them, to harm anti-Communists, and to do major disservice to their own country, what then? Do we imagine that the KGB or DGI send them along home with a lecture on loyalty?

Why should enemies of the United States not consider them "assets"? They may be undisciplined, but they cost nothing (except for Fenton), and they can be enormously effective. They may represent only a slight investment of time and effort, they are unlikely to become dangerous or do harm to the Communists, and they can be written off with ease.

They present themselves as free gifts. Why not take advantage of them? The American left is rolling in tax-exempt money, and therefore self-supporting. There need be no "paper trail" of money. These people can do great work, and may require nothing more than a bit of nudging in the right direction, some quiet coordination, and a passing of the word that they are part of the *apparat.* The latter message may be contained in the mere fact of receiving grants from hard-left sources—a kind of wink and nod, a seal of approval.

Imperfect, but free, they are good instruments of *desinformatsiya,* as raised to a fine art and instrument of policy by the Soviet government.

Yevgeny Novikov, a defector from the International Department of the Central Committee of the Communist Party of the Soviet Union, describes this sort of operation as one that would be conducted by Service A of the KGB. Commenting upon the author's remark that, too often in our own affairs, the left hand does not know what the right hand is doing, Novikov joked, "In the Soviet Union, there is only one hand."

And this is why Soviet disinformation is so well-orchestrated. It is a standard tactic, then, to generate "confirmation" by having a given "line" picked up here, there, and around the world. The "germ warfare" line of Korean War vintage shows up, even today, in Christic Comix. By the same token, the Christic line is echoed by *Geheim* in Germany, and doubtless in the Eastbloc countries as well. In time, it could turn up in Brazzaville.

It is often believed that Soviet disinformation focuses on policy and issues, rather than on personalities. This is not the case, as their spectacular operation against Franz Josef Strauss demonstrates. CIA veteran Donald Jameson described that one in detail. The object was to discredit the most capable anti-communist, so as to prevent him from rising to the position of Chancellor of West Germany. A great deal of coordination of contacts in the media, in a variety of countries, was required. The operation succeeded.

Consider that an end to *American* covert action is a standard objective of *desinformatsiya*. A leading intellectual proponent of covert action has been Theodore Shackley, author of *The Third Option,* which is said to have guided Reagan administration thinking on that subject. The contra effort was intended as a covert operation—which might have succeeded, but for the American fifth column and the waffling of Congress.

Add to this, Shackley's record of thwarting the policies of Moscow and Havana for three decades, and it is not difficult to imagine that grudges are held, and there is ample reason for use of a proxy to deliver "a kick in the gut."

On the evidence—the *real* evidence—there was no reason whatsoever for the inclusion of Shackley in the La Penca case. The question always returns, then—why did the Christics insist upon it? Was it merely Sheehan's fixation, or did he have a little help from his friends?

Who *else* wanted Singlaub's activities brought to a screeching halt? Supporting resistance to Soviet ambitions in the Philippines and Afghanistan thwarted Soviet plans. The Christic lawsuit severely crippled Jack Singlaub's anti-Communist activities for several years.

The Christics would rather be doing what they are doing than anything else they can imagine. In that respect, they are "enthusiasts." Does that prevent them from serving as surrogates of Communist imperialism?

They admit to collaboration with the Communists, and freely express their determination to protect the Communist government of Nicaragua. What they really want to "punish" is vigorous opposition to Communism.

The Christics are part of the vast network of leftist groups working quite openly on behalf of the present regime of the Nicaraguan *comandantes.* Let us assume that they do this on a volunteer basis—that the Nicaraguans have no need whatsoever to pay David MacMichael for his work on their behalf, or to compensate Quixote Center a dime for its $115 million in gifts. Only America itself can *afford* to fund its own fifth column. It is an astounding phenomenon. The rest of the world aches and cries for the opportunity to rid itself of Communist rule, while certain citizens of the freest society on earth bend every effort to preserving and extending that rule.

Such are the objectives of the alliance of some fifty leftist groups in Washington forming the so-called Central American Working Group. The La Penca lawsuit advances these objectives.

The contras were destroyed by this alliance. Is this a mere fifth column? Or is this the main column, the first column, the decisive column?

Sadly, we must score another one for this "column." Another loss, another stain, another army abandoned in the field. The Christics are proud to be part of that.

Choosing Sides

The reader has now met the plaintiffs, Avirgan and Honey, and the Christics who have taken their case and run with it. In addition, the reader has met the "major defendants."

What we see are two different sets of values in conflict, two views of the world, and, almost literally, two different generations, with the younger attacking the older.

We have seen the men who fought for the United States—in World War II, in Korea, and in Vietnam—harassed and smeared in retirement by those who refused to fight.

We have seen the courageous bushwhacked by men who have avoided, at all costs, the tests of manhood.

We have seen the loyal savaged, in the courts and in the media, by those who spend their time, in the words of Article III, Section 3 of the U.S. Constitution, "adhering to the enemy, giving them aid and comfort." Treason, we note, is the only crime defined in the Constitution.

Whose company, then, is preferable when the chips are down? On one side, we have men of proven courage, loyalty, and reliability. On the other side, we have people you cannot trust behind your back in a fight.

It comes down to that.

AFTERWORD

WHAT IS TO BE DONE?

Lenin, in 1902 published a book titled *What is to Be Done?* This rhetorical question posed by the guiding light of modern Marxism could well become the clarion call for those who would oppose legal terrorism. That is because there is much to be done. It needs to be carried out by Congress, the Executive Branch, the media, the courts, the congregations of churches and synagogues, and those citizens who actively participate in the democratic process by voting and the use of the pen to let their servant—elected officials—know how they feel about legal terrorism and the terrorists who engage in such activity.

Thomas R. Spencer, Jr., the Miami lawyer who represented General Singlaub in his legal battles with Sheehan, Avirgan and Honey has focused on the need to have Congress address the issues inherent in legal terrorism. In a July 1989 letter to members of the House and Senate, he said the following:

"In this case [Avirgan vs. Hull et al] we had lawyers, appointed by no one, responsible only to themselves, regulated by no duly elected official, acting as private attorneys general or courthouse vigilantes for purely political and financial purposes. But what is more important is that there is nothing to stop another case from creating a mockery of the judicial process. As one of the defendants put it, 'The impact of this process on innocent victims is the equivalent in terms of loss of time and money on what happens when a catastrophic illness hits a family.' Is this what we want our legal system to do via cases that judges dismiss as 'being without merit.'

"Additionally the real practical effect of the RICO statute in allowing an individual plaintiff to go back ten years is to dissolve that statute of limitations, thus creating a potpourri of problems for which statutes of limitations exist. Memories dim, papers disappear. That is the reason we have statutes of limitation.

"For all the foregoing reasons, I believe Civil RICO is in desperate need for reform, if not repeal. Indeed, Congress is in the midst of enacting legislation which may change the statute as we know it.

"As an experienced Civil RICO litigator, I have witnessed Civil RICO employed in multiple ways and improvised to fit many cases. I would like to see the 101st Congress modify RICO so that it would:

(a) require more specificity in pleading the elements of a Civil RICO action;

(b) remove the inflammatory 'Racketeer' label;

(c) allow for the timely recovery of attorneys' fees and damages for abusive litigation (and require real assurance that they will be paid);

(d) provide for limited retroactivity and limits of discovery; and

(e) increase the required 'due diligence' of the plaintiff's lawyers.

"If the recommended changes are enacted, then RICO will not become an instrument of legal terrorism to be capriciously harnessed by those who choose to resolve political differences via the courts rather than the ballot box or open debate."

Congress is moving to modify RICO but the process is tortuously slow. An intensified dialogue between the electorate and elected officials on this topic could accelerate the process of reform. The power for change clearly rests with the articulate who are dedicated enough to transform word into deed.

Relief from legal terrorism via the courts will come with glacier-like speed. On June 26, 1989 the Supreme Court rules unanimously not to limit the use of RICO. Interesting enough, four of the Justices indicated that this law is so ill-defined and vague that it might not survive a direct constitutional challenge. On the other hand, it is clear the Supreme Court does not intend to fix the RICO statutes. They see that as a task for the legislative bodies. That is why Congress is the arena in which the first steps of reform must be played out.

Other actions are also required. That reality has prompted the putting together of the following thoughts:

- The lower courts must act expeditiously to find concocted or frivolous RICO suits "as being without merit."

- The Internal Revenue Service needs to move aggressively to review the 501(c)(3) status of organizations, such as the Christics, who have been sanctioned by Rule 11 procedures in two different jurisdictions in the span of one year. Is such an organization performing a public service meriting tax exempt status? This is a question the IRS should ask itself and taxpayers might also put that question to the Service.

- The media could profit from applying a finer mesh screen to the filters used on "foreign policy conspiracy theories" before printing them. The results of the screening, when it does not support imaginative allegations, should be surfaced promptly. It is interesting to note in this context that while the La Penca story was surfaced with much fanfare in May 1986, it wasn't until July 20, 1987 that the *New York Times* wrote: "Federal agents, United States prosecutors, and spokesmen for the CIA have characterized the suit as a political fantasy. Other investigators, including reporters from major news organizations, have tried without success to find proof of aspects of the case, particularly the allegations that military supplies for the Contras may have been paid for with profits from drug trafficking."

- The CIA needs to understand that it brings no glory to itself by saying "no comment" when it is being attacked in the political arena via surrogates and has in its hands data that, imaginatively crafted to protect sources and methods, could in a pithy series of announcements debunk the fabrications of those who practice legal terrorism. In this framework, it is important to remember that the durability of CIA's institutional image for integrity is not the product of one Director. The doors of CIA headquarters at Langley, Virginia have swung open and shut for more than one man to serve at a President's pleasure.

- Members of churches and synagogues might well take note of the Elva Harper Circle technique practiced in the Grace United Methodist Church in Jacksonville, Illinois. In short, they tell their national headquarters how they want funds spent on the work of the church and not on a political agenda promoted by groups like the Christics.

It comes down to the reality that when we understand the threat of legal terrorism, we may not have a perfect counter strategy but we must do more than wring our hands and say, "What is to be done?"

BIBLIOGRAPHY

Books and Booklets

Agee, Philip. *Dirty Work*. New York: Lyle Stuart, 1979.

——— . *On the Run*. New York: Lyle Stuart, 1987.

——— . *Inside the Company: CIA Diary*. New York: Bantam, 1976.

Barron, John. *KGB: The Secret Work of Soviet Secret Agents*. New York: Reader's Digest Press, 1974.

——— . *KGB Today: The Hidden Hand*. New York: Reader's Digest Press, 1983.

Bittmann, Ladislaw. *The KGB and Soviet Disinformation*. McLean, Virginia: Pergamom Brassey's International Defense Publisher, 1985.

Borge, Tomas. *Christianity and Revolution: Tomas Borge's Theology of Life*. Orbis,

Breene, R.G. *Ordeal by Perjury: The Persecution of John Hull, The Destruction of the Contras*. San Antonio, Texas: The Faustian Society Press, 1989.

Cockburn, Leslie. *Out of Control*. New York: Atlantic Monthly Press, 1988.

Colby, William. *Lost Victory,* Chicago: Contemporary Books, 1989.

Cox, Jack. *Requiem in the Tropics*. UCA Books, 1987.

Declaration of Plaintiffs Counsel filed by Christic Institute. *Inside the Shadow Government*. Washington, DC: Christic Institute, 1988.

De La Cierva, Ricardo. *Jesuitas, Iglesia Y Marxismo 1965–1985*. 2nd ed. Barcelona, Spain: Plaza & Janes Editores, 1986.

Fredericks, Michael. *The Octopus Eagle*. Tallahassee, Florida: Loiry Publishing House, 1987.

Holt, Rod, ed. *Assault on Nicaragua: The Untold Story of the U.S. 'Secret War'*. Speeches by Daniel Sheehan and Daniel Ortega. San Francisco, California: Walnut Publishing Company, 1987.

Honey, Martha and Anthony Avirgan. *La Penca: Report of an Investigation*. Washington, DC: Christic Institute, no date.

Ledeen, Michael A. *Perilous Statecraft: An Insider's Account of the Iran-Contra Affair*. New York: Macmillian Publishing Company, 1988.

Lefevre, Ernest. *Amsterdam to Nairobi*. Ethics and Public Policy Center, 1979.

158

───────. *Nairobi to Vancouver*. Ethics and Public Policy Center, 1987.

Martin, Malachi. *The Jesuits: The Society of Jesus and the Betrayal of the Roman Catholic Church*. New York: Linden Press, 1987.

Powell, S. Steven. *Covert Cadre: Inside the Institute for Policy Studies*. Intro. David Horowitz. Ottawa, Illinois: Green Hill Publishers, Inc., 1987.

───────. *Second Front: Advancing Latin American Revolution in Washington*. Capital Research Center, 1986.

"Red Tide Rising in the Carolinas." *Western Goals Report*. Alexandria, Virginia: Western Goals, no date.

Rashke, Richard. *The Killing of Karen Silkwood*. Boston, Massachusetts: Houghton Mifflin Company, 1981.

Romerstein, Herbert and Stanislav Levchenko. *The KGB Against the "Main Enemy": How the Soviet Intelligence Service Operates against the United States*. New York: Lexington Books, 1989.

Shackley, Theodore. *The Third Option: An American View of Counterinsurgency Operations*. Reader's Digest Press, 1981.

Shultz, Richard H. and Roy Godson. *Dezinformatsia*. McLean, Virginia: Pergamon Brassey's International Defense Publishers, 1984.

Somoza, Anastasio, as told to Jack Cox, *Nicaragua Betrayed*. Western Islands, 1980.

Spence, Gerry. *Gunning for Justice*. Doubleday, 1982.

Tyson, Jas L. *Target America*. Discipleship Books, 1985.

Whalen, James and Franklin Jaeckle. *The Soviet Assault on America's Southern Flank*. Regnery, 1988.

Periodicals and Others

"A (Roger) Miranda Warning." *AIM Report*, January-A 1988.

Alterman, Eric. "Danny Sheehan." *Regardie's*, June 1988, pp. 37–40.

Bacal, Jon. "Georgetown's Nicaragua Link." *Guardian*, Georgetown University, March 1987.

Brock, David. "Christic Mystics and Their Drug Running Theories." *The American Spectator*, May 1988, pp. 22–26.

Buchanan, Patrick. "The Maligning of an American Patriot." *The Washington Times*, 29 June 1988.

Caldwell, Robert J. "Put to the Test, the Christic Case Collapsed." *The San Diego Tribune*, 3 July 1988.

Cerabino, Frank. "Contra Suit Costs Institute $1 Million." *The Miami Herald*, 4 February 1989, p. 1D.

Chardy, Alfonso. "Reagan Aides and the 'Secret' Government." *The Miami Herald*, 5 July 1987, p. F1.

"The Christic Institute: Enforcing the Brezhnev Doctrine in Central America." *Journal of Defense and Diplomacy*, Study Series No. 3.

"Christic Institute Suit Bombs." *AIM Report*, July-B 1988.

"Christic 'Lie' Probe." *Washington Inquirer*, 19 May 1989, Vol. IX. p. 1.

Clary, Mike. "A Conspiracy so Immense." *Topic: The Miami Herald Magazine*, 26 June 1988, pp. 8–19.

Codevilla, Angelo, "Political Warfare." in *Political Warfare and Psychological Operations*, eds. Carnes Lord and Frank Barnett, National Defense University Press, 1989.

"Confessions of a Media Mole." *AIM Report*, January-B 1989.

Convergence, Christic Institute,

"Document Details '62 Plans on Cuba." *Washington Post*, 27 January 1989.

Fairlie, Henry. "The Fifth Columnist." review of Alexander Cockburn's *Corruption of Empire*, *The New Republic*, 28 December 1987.

Fessier, Michael. "An American Contra." *Los Angeles Times Magazine*, 31 May 1987, pp. 8–24.

Frey, Darcy, "Contregate's Quixote." *The American Lawyer*, October 1987, pp. 145–149.

Garvin, Glenn. "Pastora Accuses Owen in Bombing." *The Washington Times*, 20 May 1987.

Hedges, Michael. "Christic Group Appeals to Charity for Appeal Funds." *Washington Times*, 14 February 1989.

———— . "Christic Must Pay its Victims $1 Million." *The Washington Times*, 6 February 1989, p. A1.

———— . "Christic's 'Fairy Tale' Lawsuit Called 'Legal Terrorism'." *The Washington Times*, 28 June 1988, p. A6.

———— . "Dismissal Sought of Civil Suit over Arms to Contras." *The Washington Times*, 16 December 1986.

———— . "Christics Lawyer Fined $100,000 for 'Frivolous' Suit." *Washington Times*, 1989.

Hendrix, Kathleen. "Arms Scandal Brings Christic Institute New Visibility." *Los Angeles Times*, 12 July 1987, p. 1.

Hinson, Hal. " 'Coverup': Agitprop Theories." *Washington Post*, 4 February 1989.

"How a PR Firm Executed the Alar Scare." *Wall Street Journal*, 3 October 1989.

Huck, Susan. "The Christic Conspiracy." *Conservative Digest,* October 1988.

————. "RICO-chet," *Chief Executive,* September-October 1989.

Ingwerson, Marshall. "Left Wing Group Depicts a Shadowy Network Operating before Iran-Contra." *The Christian Science Monitor,* 24 June 1988, p. 3.

Irvine, Reed. "Come-Uppance for the Newest McCarthyism?" *Washington Times,* 14 February 1989.

————. ed. "Soulmates: PBS and the Christics." *AIM Report.* Washington, DC: Accuracy in Media, Inc., February 1989.

Kelly, Michael. "Former CIA Official Discounts Reported Iran Arms-Contra Role." *The Baltimore Sun,* 3 February 1987.

Kincaid, Cliff. "Judge King Flays the Christic Institute." *Human Events,* 18 February 1989, pp. 5–6.

————. "The Christic Institute's Legal Terrorism." *Human Events,* 28 November 1987.

————. "Who's Really Out of Control?" *Washington Times,* 19 November 1987.

Kowet, Don. "TV: Equal Time for Everyone?" *Washington Times,* 8 June 1989.

"The Left in Disneyland." *The Washington Times,* 30 June 1988.

Lessner, Richard. "Christic Turn Conspiracy Theory into a Money Cow." *Arizona Republic,* 11 July 1988.

"Liberals Respond Warily to Christics' Pleas for Aid." *Legal Times,* 27 February 1989.

Lofton, John. "Pursuit of the Christic Snark." *The Washington Times,* 15 July 1988.

Lyons, James. "Religious 'Rainmaker' Mounts Latest Crusade." *Legal Times,* 5 January 1987, pp. 2–3.

Marcus, Noreen. "U.S. Judge: Christics Owe $1 Million." *Miami Review,* 8 February 1989, p. 4.

Mark, Michael. "Court House Terrorism." *Military,* April 1989.

McGrory, Mary. "The Contra-Drug Stink." *The Washington Post,* 10 April 1988, p. B1.

"Media Blind to Leftist McCarthyism." *AIM Report,* March-A 1989.

"Media Conspirators in the Courts." *National Review,* 10 March 1989.

"Papers Show 1962 U.S. Plan Against Castro." *New York Times,* 27 January 1989.

The Presbyterian Layman, issues from November-December 1988 through July-August 1989.

"RICO Backfires," *Wall Street Journal,* 2 March 1989.

Ridge, James. "An Appeal to Reason." *Village Voice,* 5 July 1988.

"Sandinista Lovers in the Media." *AIM Report,* July-B 1986.

Schneider, Keith. "A Liberal Group Makes Waves With Its Contra Lawsuit." *The New York Times,* 20 July 1987.

Shackley, Theodore. " 'I Was Not a Participant in the Iran Weapons Transfer'." *The Washington Post,* 2 February 1987.

————— . "Legal Terrorism." *Defense and Diplomacy,* December 1987, pp. 8–9.

Shepard, Scott. "Suit Contends U.S. Foreign Policy has been Taken Over by Renegades." *Atlanta Constitution,* 24 April 1988, p. A1.

Silverstein, Ken. "Does the Christic Institute's Case Hold Up?" *Interview,* Vol. XVIII, no. 4, pp. 107 & 132.

Tomb, Geoffrey, "It's Left vs. Right for Funds." *The Miami Herald,* 25 February 1989, p. B1.

Traub, James. "The Law and the Prophet." *Mother Jones,* February/March 1988, pp. 21–48.

Volksy, George. "U.S. Judge Dismisses Suit by Two Journalists in 1984 Nicaraguan Bombing." *New York Times,* 24 June 1988.

Waller, Michael, "Contras' Accusers Fall Apart Under Scrutiny." *West Watch,* November 1987.

Weist, Jeff. "Inside CAHI." *Guardian,* Georgetown University, March 1987.

Wisdom, Alan. "The Christic Institute: Fighting the 'Secret Team'—With Your Church's Money." *Religion & Democracy,* November 1988, pp. 1–2.

Wolin, Merie Linda. "Roots of Revolution: Influences on Tomas Borge." *Los Angeles Herald,* 5 May 1985.

INDEX

166

Waller, James (Dr.), 124
Wall Street Journal, 5-6, 84, 92
Walsh, Lawrence, 141
Warburg, James P., 104
Warner Theater, 98
Washington Post, 33, 43, 58, 84, 92
Webb, Lee, 108
Weinberger, Caspar, 70, 121
Weiner, Jon, 117
Weiss, Cora, 10
Weiss, Marc, 36
Weiss, Peter, 29, 149
Welch, Richard, 49
Westover, Peter, 13
"West 57th Street", 93, 135
What is to Be Done?, 153
Wheaton deposition, 86-87
Wheaton, Eugene, 86-87, 117, 139
Wheaton, Phil (Rev.), 78-79, 113
Wheaton, Sue, 78-79, 113
White Panther Party, 83
White, Robert, 117

Wickwire, Chester (Rev.), 79
Wilcox, Leo, 32
Willow Grove Naval Air Station, 15
Willson, Brian, 50
Wilson, Leland (Rev.), 112-113
Winsor, Curtin, 21-22
Wodka, Steve, 34
Wolf, Louis, 49-50, 69, 78-79, 150
Wolin, Linda, 119-120
"Woodstock" generation, 99
World Anti-Communist League, 59, 88
World Bank, 16
World Council of Churches, 119
World Peace Council, 149
Wounded Knee, 31

Yorkin Foundation, 110
Yorkin, Peg, 110
Youth Project, 102-103, 108, 110-111

Zanzibar, 15
Z (film), 29
Z. Smith Reynolds Foundation, 108